MySpace
Unraveled

A Parent's Guide
to Teen Social Networking
from the Directors of BlogSafety.com

Larry Magid and Anne Collier

MySpace Unraveled:

What it is and how to use it safely

Larry Magid

Anne Collier

Peachpit Press

1249 Eighth Street, Berkeley, CA 94710

510/524-2178 • 800/283-9444 • 510/524-2221 (fax)

Find us on the Web at: www.peachpit.com

To report errors, please send a note to errata@peachpit.com

Published by Peachpit Press, a division of Pearson Education

Project Editor: Cliff Colby

Editor: Jill Marts Lodwig

Production Editor: Connie Jeung-Mills

Copyeditor: Kathy Simpson

Compositor: Interactive Composition Corporation

Indexer: James Minkin

Cover Design and Production: Charlene Charles Will

Cover Images: All images iStock.com. Top row, left to right: Puthathai Chungyam, Nancy Louie, Paul Piebinga, James Boulette, James Pauls, [information not available], Jacob Wackerhausen. Bottom row, left to right: [information not available], Paul Piebinga, [information not available], Trevor Nielson, Jason Stitt, Galina Barskaya, Jason Stitt.

ISBN 0-321-48018-X

9 8 7 6 5 4 3 2

Printed and bound in the United States of America

Dedication

To Patti and Ron

Acknowledgments

No project like this would be possible were it not for the support of our families. A special thank you to Ron Collier and Patti Regehr Magid for their patience, understanding, and support. There were weeks when Anne and Larry spent more time with each other than they did with their respective spouses and families. Thanks also to Sam and Will Collier, for being good critical thinkers and safe online socializers and for allowing "Mom" to be "author" for awhile, and to Katherine Magid and Will Magid, both recent graduates of teenage-hood, for providing sage advice as social-networking experts who don't have to reach too far back to remember what it's like to be a teen. Thanks also to our young friends Susan, Cameron, Lisa, and many anonymous teen participants in the BlogSafety forum for serving as our native guides in the world of teen social networking.

We are indebted to Danah Boyd at the University of California, Berkeley, for glimpses into her pioneering research on social networking, and also to the researchers at the University of New Hampshire's Crimes Against Children Research Center, the Pew Internet & American Life Project, and the Kaiser Family Foundation. They keep all of us current on children's use of the Web and digital media.

We want to acknowledge Detective Frank Dannahey for sharing his wise, balanced approach to working with online kids, and Stephen Carrick-Davies of London-based Childnet International for his support, advice, and encouragement and for helping us understand some of the international implications of social networking. Thanks also to President Ernie Allen and our many friends at the National Center for Missing & Exploited Children for their support and inspiring work. They are great champions for our children.

This book never could have happened if it weren't for the steady, eagle-eyed editorial supervision of Jill Marts Lodwig, copy editor Kathy Simpson, production editor Connie Jeung-Mills, and the tireless contributions of Mona Bueler who helped us with the hands-on sections of this book. Thanks also to Peachpit Press's Cliff Colby and Nancy Ruenzel for encouraging us to embark on this project.

While we were writing this book, we were also in the final stages of launching BlogSafety.com, a web forum (operated by the non-profit Tech Parenting Group) where parents, teens and experts are talking with each other about the promises and challenges of social networking. Although the site, like this book, is editorially independent, it is receiving support from sponsoring companies, including MySpace, AOL, Bebo, Facebook, Friendster, Hi5, SixApart/LiveJournal, Tagged and Xanga, as well as our hosting company, LiveWorld. These companies agreed to put aside their competitive differences to support a project dedicated to making the Web safer for children and teens, and we appreciate their support.

Although MySpace officials didn't review our manuscript and had no editorial control or influence, we are grateful for their technical support, their insight into the inner workings of the company, and their willingness to answer questions, especially as they were changing some of MySpace's privacy policies as we were finishing the book. Special thanks to Hemanshu Nigam, chief security officer of Fox Interactive Media, and MySpace executives Shawn Gold and Sarah Kaleel for their advice and technical assistance.

Contents

CHAPTER 1

Online Socializing Basics

WELCOME TO WEB 2.0—the everywhere, all-the-time, multi-media, multidevice, downloadable *and* uploadable, user-driven Internet. Although many of us may not be aware of all the Web's capabilities these days, rest assured that our teens are. Not only have they figured out Web 2.0, but they're also among its most experienced producers, videographers, DJs, VJs, publishers, podcasters, and mobloggers (mobile bloggers).

Of course, teenagers aren't necessarily aware of all the Web knowledge they possess. They don't really think about whether they're creating multimedia and socializing online or offline. They just produce and socialize, using tools that happen to involve the Internet, such as instant messaging, blogs, chat, texting on phones, and social networking.

What *Is* Social Networking?

Social networking wasn't coined by teens; they don't use the term to describe their online activities. Young people just socialize. They update their profiles, post comments, blog, add friends (like buddies on a buddy list), and chat on what have become known by us adults as social-networking sites.

As we adults struggle to find the language that describes this phenomenon, teens are speeding ahead, making it up as they go, including the language and the tools and their uses. To them, these sites are just another tool for socializing. Sometimes, teens call these sites *online communities,* but for most of them, the line between online and offline is decidedly blurred.

Trying to define social networking is very much like trying to pin down a moving target, because it's evolving so quickly. In its earliest phase, social networking was either blogging (having an online journal or being an amateur commentator) or socializing (finding friends and connecting with them).

A *blog* (short for *Web log*) is simply a Web page anyone can create without any technical know-how. Blogs were and still are easy to do because companies have created tools that are very much like word-processing applications. By simply typing words onscreen and dragging photos from their hard drives to the page, bloggers ushered in the era of desktop publishing for the Web: All of a sudden, anyone could post a Web page, and teenagers did so with a vengeance.

A parallel development was the pure social networking (more about connecting than personal punditry) that started in the '90s but really took off in 2003 with Friendster.com (**FIGURE 1.1**).

Meanwhile, blogging kept getting more interactive and adding more features, with young people fueling this process. They have made it as much about casual communication and socializing as it is about publishing and journaling. The teen version of blogging is now better described as social networking. Adult pundits, researchers, hobbyists, and many teens to this day continue to do the old kind of blogging: blogging with reader feedback (and now photos).

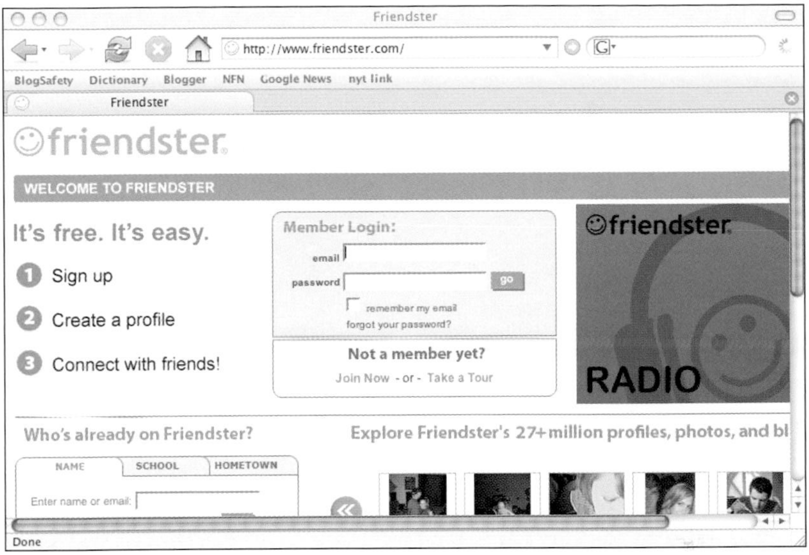

FIGURE 1.1 Friendster was one of the original social-networking sites.

Creative Networking

MySpace was the turning point for social networking. Unlike Friendster, which arrived on the scene at about the same time, it allowed users to combine the media-rich self-expression that blogging was beginning to offer with multiple socializing tools (IM, email, comments, buddy lists, discussion boards, and chat). Suddenly, there was something seemingly made to order for teens. You could call it creative networking or social producing—maybe even collective self-expression.

Friendster, to be fair, has since added a bunch of self-expression features, but it was MySpace's embrace of both publishing and socializing tools— when it mattered, when teens were looking for something even more social than blogs—that made it a traffic-growth record-breaker (**FIGURE 1.2**).

By mid-2005, within two years of MySpace's debut as a social-networking site, *Business Week* reported that MySpace was getting more page views than Google, and by early 2006, MySpace was welcoming around 200,000 new members a day. Overnight, it seemed, the site's population was bigger than the world's most-populated cities.

FIGURE 1.2 MySpace ushered in social producing and creative networking.

The New York Times and *The Wall Street Journal* have described MySpace as a combination of an alternate-reality game, a nightclub with lots of beautiful people and wannabes, MTV, and a teenager's bedroom—a place where, as the *Times* put it, "grownups are an alien species" ("Do You MySpace?" by Alex Williams, August 28, 2005).

In other words, teens took the site's name literally: It was *their* space. Grownups—especially parents—were not even on the radar screen of the average MySpace user. Despite growing evidence that parents were checking out their kids' MySpace activities, young people were in denial.

Part of what made MySpace so fun for them was the very fact that parents weren't there; it was *teen* space, very much like their own rooms with the door closed or a party when parents are out of town. Yes, it was public, but "private" in a way—something like when kids go off to college. And MySpace held another contradiction that teens like: "safe" (anonymous) but with just enough riskiness to make it cool, and individual but also delightfully collective.

Young people today have more awareness of the public aspect of social networking, of course. But back to its appeal. . .

MySpace—in fact, the whole Web now—is basically whatever anybody wants it to be. And this is the key to understanding teens and Web 2.0: MySpace, social networking, and Web 2.0 in general are different experiences for everyone who uses them. Why? Because teenagers use MySpace for different things.

Profiles: The New 'Chat'

Some teens spend all their MySpace time checking comments on their profiles and commenting on their friends' profiles, noting how their photos are ranked, and where they're ranked on their friends' "Top Friends" lists. In these cases, MySpace is purely social.

KEY PARENTING POINT

We parents can understand the social Web much better by talking with our own kids about how they use it, rather than relying on reading news stories about it.

Designing and Decorating Spaces

Other teens are into visual self-expression. How you decorate your space says a lot about you. Some teens change background music, graphics, fonts, photos, and links often; it's a lot easier than redecorating one's bedroom, and a lot more people see it.

Creating a profile is also a way to experiment with identity—something teenagers do a lot and something psychologists say they're supposed to be doing. For some MySpace users, though, profile customization isn't just about visuals; it's also a way of showing off their technical sophistication. MySpace lets people add to their spaces software code they've written or downloaded from other sites, such as PimpMySpace.org and MySpaceCode.com. With this special code, people can add effects like glittery text, animations, clip art, and *avatars* (animated representations of themselves).

A Public Journal

For some MySpace users, the space is all about blogging or being a writer—updating their online journals every day, every week, or whenever the spirit moves them. It's like an online diary, which is a bit of an oxymoron, because this "diary" is far from private. Some users try to gain at least a little control over who reads their entries, however, by registering as 14- or 15-year-olds, in which case they have the option of letting only people on their friends lists see what they write (though MySpace is expected to change this policy soon, so that anyone can go private). Some parents and law-enforcement people aren't crazy about that.

Interest Communities

MySpace has all sorts of communities.

There are very personal ones, like the people on a user's friends list, and absurdly giant personal communities, like the people on the friends list of someone who's planning to win a virtual popularity contest.

There are also macro interest communities, such as the Music, Film, Books, and Games groups. Of these, the largest by far is Music, the original MySpace community. For a lot of MySpacers, that community is what the site is all about.

Then there are groups one can join to talk about things like hobbies, sports, politics, and parenting (yes, there are parenting groups on MySpace!).

Even entire high schools have created their own communities, run by a student moderator who has been designated by participants.

As with all technologies, there are an upside and a downside to online communities. Teens can learn a lot in groups about things like national politics. For example, we have a 17-year-old Nevada friend who participates in a group moderated by a young person in Washington, D.C. But negative or destructive interests can also be reinforced in an online community; see Chapters 5 and 6 for more on the risks of social networking and how it can be done safely.

Teens' blogs and social-networking spaces are just online extensions or representations of themselves and their lives, with an intriguing, unsettling dose of good ol' Internet anonymity thrown in to keep things interesting.

A Parents'-Eye View

MySpace profiles can be pretty jarring to parents when they check out the site for the first time.

The profiles may have a disheveled look, in the way that kids and their rooms sometimes look to adults. Then there are the photos, some of which seem over the top to parents thinking about who else is viewing them. You may have seen this effect in local TV news stories, in what sometimes seems like a ratings grab: the shocked looks on parents' faces when a reporter takes them to a page of search results displaying profiles of teens from the high school their children attend.

What parents are seeing, in effect, is what adolescents have been doing and saying for eons in more private spaces like the local malt shop, college keg parties, the mall, or behind the bleachers at a football game on a Friday night.

What's very different here is that all the "Ps"—peers, parents, predators, police, and policymakers—are thrown into the same space, which makes for a volatile potion! It's definitely shaking up adults.

What we need to keep in mind is that these kinds of teen self-expression have been going on for generations and that the content is not always "real." It's an act in a lot of cases. Remember? We experimented with who we were when we were at parties too. We're not saying everybody on MySpace is acting out, showing off, or experimenting with personas. Not even all the teenagers are, of course.

Teens Are Figuring It Out

OK, so experimenting with who they are is typical teenage fare.

"But it's *public*," you may say.

Exactly. That's what teen social networkers have been in denial about: that we parents can actually *watch* them at this giant party.

Adults aren't the only ones who have been affected by all the media coverage of MySpace, however. Teens are becoming very aware that this isn't a truly private space where they can let their hair down away from adult scrutiny.

This growing awareness is both good and bad from a parent's perspective. The really good news is that kids are getting smarter. They know that what they post on MySpace and other social-networking sites can be exploited by peers and strangers, and that they can lose control of what they upload. Comments, photos, and videos can be copied and pasted in other Web sites, shared on file-sharing networks, and passed around in IMs and emails.

KEY PARENTING POINT

If you suspect that your kids don't know, by all means ask them if they're careful about what they say and upload on MySpace, and whether they've been harassed by peers or strangers and how they handled it.

FIGURE 1.3 Xanga is No. 2 in popularity among 12- to 17-year-olds, according to the latest figures from online research firm eMarketer.

FIGURE 1.4 Facebook, in eMarketer's Top 6 social-networking sites, is represented on every four-year college and university campus in the United States.

The bad news about this growing awareness of adult scrutiny is that young MySpace users may just move on. Although it might seem strange to consider this bad news, keep in mind that there are zillions of other social-networking sites where kids can go (**FIGURES 1.3** and **1.4**). And many of these sites are less accountable, at least to shareholders. In fact, some of them, like myYearbook.com, are teeny private companies started by high-school students on their spring break (**FIGURE 1.5**). All these options make it all the more difficult for parents to keep track of their teens' online activities. And the number of these sites is only increasing.

Multiplying Like Rabbits

The sites we hear about in the news and Nielsen/NetRatings' Top 10 barely scratch the surface of community sites where kids can register for free from home or anywhere there's an Internet connection.

Wikipedia.org, the collaborative online encyclopedia, links to nearly 5 dozen in its list of "notable social-networking sites."

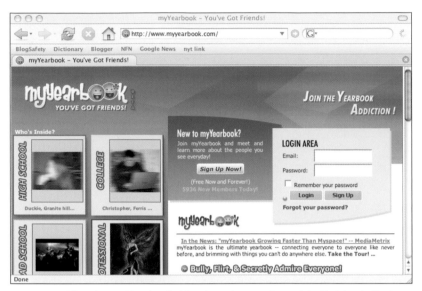

FIGURE 1.5 The site myYearbook, No. 4 on the comScore Media Metrix list in December '05, was started by high-school students on their spring break.

KEY PARENTING POINT

It might be informative to check out some of these other social networks to see how people use them and then ask your children whether they use more than one. An 18-year-old American au pair in The Netherlands whom we've interviewed told us she maintains pages on MySpace, LiveJournal, and Xanga because different friends use these sites, and she wants to be able to stay in touch with all of them.

There are narrow-interest sites revolving around specific music genres; geographically oriented sites (from metro areas to whole countries); counterculture sites; teen-only sites; social-elite, invitation-only sites; college-oriented sites; brand-related sites hosted by marketers. . . the list goes on.

The Federal Bureau of Investigation said in May 2006 that it had a list of some 200 social-networking sites (though it's not sharing its list with the public). We believe that the FBI's number is conservative, because Web users soon will be able to create their own social-networking sites if they want to, just as they can now create their own Web pages, blogs, podcasts, and *vlogs* (video blogs).

Social networking is also happening all over the world. Swedish, Korean, Portuguese, Chinese, Estonian, and Indian parents have a lot of the same questions and concerns we have, except that they concern Lunarstorm.se, Cyworld.com, Orkut.com, QQ.com, Connect.ee, and Hi5.com, to name just a few top sites in other countries (**FIGURES 1.6** through **1.9**).

FIGURE 1.6 More than 90 percent of Sweden's high-school students are members of Lunarstorm, according to the *International Herald Tribune.*

FIGURE 1.7 Orkut is a hugely popular Google site in Brazil; 11 million of its 15 million users socialize there.

FIGURE 1.8 Connect.ee is a popular social-networking site in Estonia.

FIGURE 1.9 Hi5 is a San Francisco-based social-networking site that's a favorite among young Net users in India.

Teen social networking is, in effect, beyond control except maybe in individual homes.

Even at home, we can say "no more MySpace," but you can see that there are burgeoning alternatives and work-arounds in and beyond the home. Laws and filters can try to block them in specific spaces, such as federally funded schools and libraries. But with wireless broadband

Internet connections now or soon available anywhere via phones, game players, video music players, PDAs, and laptops, the reach of these automated parental controls is diminishing rather than expanding.

We online-safety advocates have been saying for more than a decade that there is no substitute for engaged parenting. Well, we are saying it louder now. But that engagement, as you'll discover throughout this book is less about control than it is about communication.

Not Their Parents' Web

We need to understand that the Web, as our teenagers use it, is not just a productivity tool or a more convenient way to find information—not even a way to share photos with distant relatives. It's not a tool as we adults see it. It's an extension of teenagers themselves.

Fast Company magazine recently interviewed Evan Rifkin, co-founder of TagWorld.com, a rapidly up-and-coming "social networking plus media hosting" site. Rifkin said in that interview, published in the June 2006 issue, "People want to live their lives online." This is, in fact, what's happening with our kids, for whom the distinction between online and offline is blurring rapidly, as we mentioned earlier.

Because of its flexibility and all the different forms of interaction and self-expression MySpace allows, young people are able to move their lives online too. Just as water finds outlets and cracks that we never knew about, teenagers found MySpace.

CHAPTER 2

The Scene

EXACTLY WHAT ARE TEENS *doing* on these sites? If you ask them, they'll most likely tell you they're "just hanging out."

Hanging out on MySpace and other social-networking sites is sort of like networking in the adult sense of the word, except that teens aren't reaching out to their extended network of friends with some purpose in mind, as we think of it. Instead, they're engaged in conveniently asynchronous but also real-time collective and interactive self-expression. Whew—it's not easy being a teenager!

Let's take a look at what this self-expression is all about, from teens' and the experts' points of view.

Creating a Self, Online

MySpace profiles represent teenagers' *online selves*—not so much an extension of who they are but who they see themselves to be at the moment, expressed in comments, photos, and music (**FIGURE 2.1**).

FIGURE 2.1 The MySpace profiles of 17-year-old "Cameron."

"With MySpace, you can get more creative about who you are," says Lisa, an 18-year-old MySpace user in California. "When you're a teenager, that's what you're trying to do."

Part of what forms those online selves, in addition to profiles, are friends' photos and comments that appear on the same page. The combination of all these elements, which is very much a group activity, presents a self defined in relation to others (**FIGURE 2.2**).

A lot of thought often goes into these profiles, in what looks to adults like terse comments and crazy photos. This haphazardness is a natural

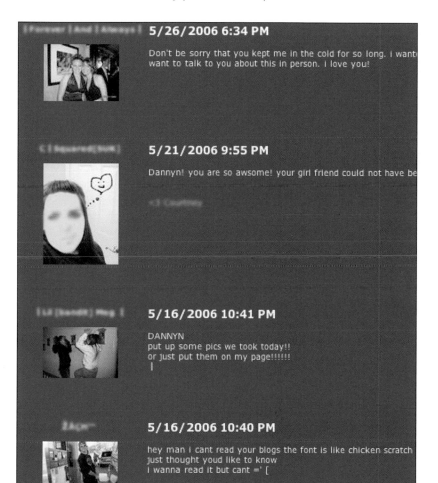

5/26/2006 6:34 PM

Don't be sorry that you kept me in the cold for so long. i want want to talk to you about this in person. i love you!

5/21/2006 9:55 PM

Dannyn! you are so awsome! your girl friend could not have be

5/16/2006 10:41 PM

DANNYN
put up some pics we took today!!
or just put them on my page!!!!!!
I

5/16/2006 10:40 PM

hey man i cant read your blogs the font is like chicken scratch just thought youd like to know
i wanna read it but cant =' [

FIGURE 2.2 Friends' comments on Cameron's page.

byproduct of teens' making up who they are as they go along. Although it may look aimless and superficial, it's actually very productive, says Danah Boyd, a pioneering social-networks researcher at the University of California, Berkeley. MySpace is "not the waste of time adults think it is. What's happening in it is what academics call *informal learning*," Boyd says.

Hanging out has a lot of social value, adds Boyd. "It's where you learn social norms, rules, how to interact with others, narrative [writing a blog], personal and group history, and media literacy."

David Huffaker, a researcher of online social behavior at Northwestern University, agrees. "These activities are important for identity exploration, which is one of the principal tasks of adolescence," Huffaker he wrote in an academic paper, "Teen Blogs Exposed: The Private Lives of Teens Made Public" which he presented at the American Association for the Advancement of Science in February 2006.

Detective Frank Dannahey, a 15-year veteran Youth Division police officer in Rocky Hill, Connecticut, has worked and consulted on a lot of social-networking cases. He takes a pragmatic approach to MySpace, based on his conversations with teens: "For the most part, these [MySpace users] are just average, everyday, good kids. . . and this is part of their social life."

How Public Is It?

To get a sense of how differently adult visitors and teen users perceive the public aspect of MySpace, picture a giant big-city train station full of people—say, Penn Station in Manhattan.

A person entering the station for the first time might take a sweeping look around, feel intimidated, and look for the nearest exit. A New York City commuter, on the other hand, would simply zip in and head straight for her train.

A socializing teenager entering MySpace is much like that commuter: He'll pop in and make a beeline for his friends, who are gathering in a group under the Departures sign, where they *always* meet. He'll check for messages, look for the latest comments or blog postings, and type his reactions and comments.

By contrast, we parents go into MySpace very new to this phenomenon, maybe searching for a child's high school or just randomly clicking profiles (**FIGURE 2.3**). Quickly overwhelmed by the vulnerability that goes with exposing oneself in such a massive public space, we might develop a sudden urge to head for the exit—and insist that our kids do the same.

FIGURE 2.3 Thousands of MySpacers' profiles are just a click away.

But kids rarely use MySpace that way; they don't wander aimlessly, for the most part. When they've finished checking and updating their own profiles, they usually check their friends' profiles. "If they're really, really,

really bored, *maybe* they'll start random searching," says Boyd. But teens don't search the way adults do, in a sweeping, random, out-of-the-blue fashion. Kids first search for people with shared interests, via their friends' profiles and friends lists, and then search their friends' friends lists and out through the concentric circles as time allows (**FIGURE 2.4**).

FIGURE 2.4 If there's searching at all, it starts with their friends list, ground zero for teen social networkers.

Purposeful, Not Random

That's how our 17-year-old friend Cameron (not his real name) in Nevada describes it. He uses MySpace to stay in touch with friends in his and his girlfriend's high schools, as well as to discuss national politics in a group run by "someone in DC" who keeps the conversation going and to discuss soccer in a group moderated by a soccer player in Europe.

He says those activities are all he has time for, because in addition to being a student, he's on a soccer team and works part-time for a veterinarian. He doesn't have time to customize his profile or bother with background music.

"I don't blog either. I'm not really into sharing my inner thoughts in public," says Cameron. "But I don't have any privacy tools turned on, because then people like my cousin in Texas couldn't find me."

Lisa, the MySpace user in California, is more focused on profiles and hasn't spent as much time in groups as Cameron has. She did join a MySpace group that is an online version of a real-life group she's a member of: the National Young Leaders Conference. This was pure practicality.

"All the kids in my class involved in [the conference] couldn't always coordinate their schedules to get together at the same time. So we formed a community on MySpace to keep our meeting minutes," Lisa says. Now there's no more "You must've missed the meeting!"

Multisocializing

But even though all this happens on MySpace, this is not to say that social networking is happening only there. We're seeing more and more reports around the country about teen multisocializing, which is like multitasking but encompasses a whole lot more than just socializing. *Multisocializing* describes how kids simultaneously juggle devices (such as PCs, phones, game players, and MP3 players), technologies (such as IM, phone texting, and MySpace), people or conversations, and tasks like homework while they are socializing.

Teenagers have many layers and shades of communication styles, depending on who's involved, and what device or site is handy.

Lisa, who uses social-networking site Facebook more now that she's heading to college, says she didn't use MySpace for discussion boards or chat. Instead, she used eSPINtheBottle.com (maybe because it's for teens only), where she'd chat with Mike in Florida. For her, different sites are for different types of communication, as well as for different types of friends.

"I've known Mike online since I was 14," she says. "I met him completely by accident when I was looking for a CliffsNotes–type site. For some reason, his Web site popped up when I was on that site, so I met him in chat on it."

She's been talking to him online off and on ever since. She has "talked with him on the phone only once or twice. I have no intention of meeting him in person." When she does talk or text on the phone, she uses these types of communication for different purposes. The former are more for short, to-the-point purposes like arranging a meeting place, the latter for more sustained, multiconversation socializing.

While MySpace too is used for multisocializing—sometimes for recording meeting minutes; sometimes for talking about the World Cup—most of the time, it's just used for hanging out. Even so, it is very purposeful, in the sense that teens need to do these kinds of things as they develop their own identities. None of it is as public as it looks to a parent or any other adult coming in and just browsing around.

Many Little Worlds

Of course, all this socializing isn't one-on-one. It's happening in the many social groups—tight and exclusive or random and easygoing—that form in middle school and high school. It helps to think back to our own high-school days. We had groups of various sizes and levels of intimacy. Even then, there were "jocks" and "freaks," maybe even "dweebs," but there were also Astronomy Club and the tennis team and the cheerleading squad. A person might've dipped into and identified with several groups, and found real support and validation in one, but the groups didn't really mix it up. They just coexisted. That's what it's like on MySpace (**FIGURE 2.5**).

Cameron's high-school friends talk about their school stuff in their MySpace profiles—people, events, parties, and so on. These discussions are separate from his soccer and politics groups. Boyd refers to this as "little communities. . . multiple publics" all coexisting in one giant space with zippo contact—the groups teens form and turn to for support and mutual learning in the process of learning about themselves.

"I found an entire community of Christian rock culture," says Boyd, "and they're hanging out on the same Web site [MySpace] with a whole

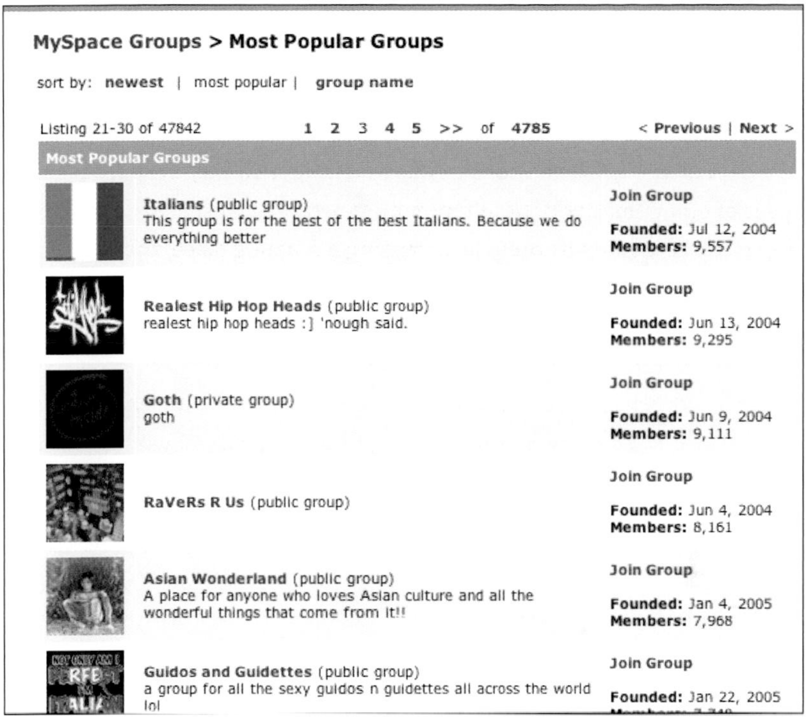

FIGURE 2.5 MySpace has thousands upon thousands of social groups of every imaginable makeup.

group of gangsta kids—no interaction whatsoever. Adults come in and see and react to all this [together in one space] when there's actually nothing to react to, because [the teens] probably don't even know about each other."

Mom and Dad might browse the profiles of kids who go to Suzy's high school. They might see some pretty racy or compromising party photos and think, "Look at these people our daughter is associating with!" Yet more than likely, Suzy is not socializing with them at all. Her profile's just on the same site as theirs. That doesn't mean they'd be in the same *physical* space together. It's possible that they could be at the same place on a Saturday night, but for the sake of rational parent–child communication, it would work better (and be more realistic) if Suzy's parents didn't make that assumption.

What we're seeing when we browse MySpace is a *whole lot* of the little communities that teens naturally form, try out, and sometimes depend on as they work out who they are. Young people are very focused on these communities as they socialize online, and this is a much safer way to use MySpace than the way adults approach it or think that teens approach it.

Acting Up in Public

Believe it or not, something MySpace reminds us of (and we're dating ourselves here) is Arnold's—everybody's favorite burger joint in the TV show "Happy Days."

As we aged viewers might remember, Arnold's is where Richie, Joanie, the Fonz, and everyone else who mattered ate, chatted, flirted, and exhibited plenty of youthful sexuality—tempered, of course, by the mores of a sitcom set in the '50s. Although some adults were usually in the restaurant, they were back in a corner minding their own business (and maybe rolling their eyeballs). No one else existed when the teen "owners" of that space occupied it.

This naturally egocentric, nothing-else-exists teenage approach lives on in the 21st century—the age of exposure. But now, many people are watching teens behave as though nothing else exists. It's a contradiction, and a very interesting one: Consciously, today's teenagers seem to think that no one is out there watching, but at the subconscious level, they put on a lot of performances for that nonaudience.

The explanation might be the media environment they've grown up in. Consider the amazing time we live in. "Paris Hilton is famous because she's famous," Boyd points out. The idols of "American Idol" are instantly famous, and the show's ratings suggest that everybody else should want to be famous, too. There are plenty more reality TV shows that are all about exposing the intimate details of people's lives—including "real" celebrities of all sorts.

"Kids are getting all these messages saying, 'Expose, expose, expose,' " Boyd says. "If you don't, your friends will expose you. We're all living in a superpublic environment, getting the message that you have more power if you expose yourself than if someone else exposes you."

You can make a fairly direct correspondence between "American Idol" and MySpace when you consider photo rankings and how important the number of comments and the length of friends lists can be. MySpace is just a reflection of the everyday media environment.

That's not to say every teenager likes that environment. A teen posted in our forum, BlogSafety.com, that she found MySpace "really boring—just a big popularity contest." She was referring to the vying to be among friends' "Top 8," the photo rankings, the cachet of having long friends lists and lots of comments, and so on (**FIGURE 2.6**). She left MySpace. Other dissenters, such as Cameron, just ignore this aspect of the site and get on with keeping up with the busy lives of their friends.

FIGURE 2.6 Another exhaustive friends' list on MySpace.

Our point is that MySpace is the new burger joint, only infinitely bigger and more diverse. The same stuff is going on. But instead of one or two social groups, there are thousands upon thousands, and instead of an ignored group of adults in the back corner, there are tens of millions, both on MySpace and looking in on it.

KEY PARENTING POINT

We welcome a discussion on teen social networking and related issues—with teens and parents—at BlogSafety.com, our new forum about Web 2.0 and teens. We're all pioneers on the social Web, where privacy, safety, and parenting are concerned. If teens disagree with us, we'd welcome their reactions in the forum! If parents have questions, fellow parents (and teenagers and safety advocates) are there to answer them. BlogSafety is social networking about social networking—a Web 2.0-style solution.

Are They Overexposed?

Of course that's the fear: Our teenagers are way overexposed as they socialize on the Net. But think for a moment about the atmosphere in which we're all living right now and how that might be shaping our thoughts about kids on MySpace.

There's a "war on terrorism" going on. Reportedly, there's a pandemic approaching. In the spring of 2006, "Dateline NBC" couldn't seem to stop airing shows featuring sexual predators, while local papers across the country were beginning to pick up on the trend and running stories about predators on MySpace. We need to remember that "what goes wrong is news," as *New York Times* political reporter Elisabeth Bumiller wrote in "The White House Without a Filter" (June 6, 2006). It's a good idea to take what the news media and politicians say about social networking with a good-sized grain of salt.

"Fear is a very important emotion," says Boyd, who is often quoted as someone trying to *assuage* fears. It alerts us to risk, she adds, "and how to assess it." That's true for everybody, but psychologists tell us it's also one of the principal tasks of adolescent development: risk assessment. It's something they need to do.

Even so, every generation of parents wishes it could eliminate all risk from children's lives. And every generation of teens engages in behaviors that make parents have that wish.

A few generations ago, parents fretted over the jitterbug. In the '50s, parents worried about the sexually charged influence of rock 'n' roll. Parents in the '60s worried that experimentation with marijuana would lead their kids into lives of depravity, but somehow, those kids—the Baby Boomers—not only survived, but also managed to grow up to run companies, universities, media empires, and the country itself.

We're not being cavalier. We're just saying that social networking is today's fear of choice. But as in every generation, despite a few casualties, the vast majority of these "users" of a different sort are not being harmed even emotionally, much less physically.

We suspect that today's young people will survive this new "threat." In fact, we're confident that the positive aspects of social networking far outweigh the dangers, and based on what we now see among high-school and college students, it's clear to us that the vast majority of kids using these sites will be just fine.

And they'll be in even better shape if they consider one important caveat: If teenagers are still in denial about the social networks being their own space, they need to come out of denial. Increasingly, college admissions offices, prospective employers, and other people whom they want to impress are searching MySpace and other such sites—not just general Web search engines—for information about them.

What young people put in their profiles and blogs can not only be found by people other than their friends, they can be printed out and filed online and on hard drives, passed along in emails and IMs, and copied and shared on file-sharing networks or third-party Web sites (more about this in Chapter 5). Social networkers soon will soon need spin-doctor skills as they negotiate this "superpublic" cyberspace.

CHAPTER 3

MySpace for Parents

Now it's time to actually try out MySpace. We don't expect most parents to become diehard MySpace fanatics (though some might), but we do hope that you'll at least sign up (it's free), create a profile, and check out a few of the features so you can see what's going on.

This chapter takes a hands-on, "cookbook" approach to using MySpace. We hope it will help you understand what the different features do and why people use them, while injecting some cautionary notes. Some of the things we'll show you include basics like how to set up a MySpace account, how to build and edit a profile, how to integrate music and video into your profile, and how to use MySpace's privacy features.

The idea, here, is for parents to get enough of a feel for the service to better understand how their kids are using it and advise them on safe, smart socializing. Although we do walk you through everything you need to know to use the service (and even make it sing and dance a little), we'll be the first to admit that this book probably won't turn the average parent into a highly sophisticated MySpace user. That's not our goal.

Our goal is to help you get your feet wet, splash around the pool, have a little fun, and maybe swim a lap or two. After all, if your kids are going to be swimming in the deep end, you should know the layout of the pool.

In Chapter 4, we cover some of the ways MySpace helps manage a user's social life. Then, in Chapter 7, we take you on a tour of some of MySpace's more advanced features. Don't worry—there won't be a quiz, and we don't expect you to master every feature we talk about!

Setting Up an Account

Setting up a basic MySpace account is fast and easy. Follow these steps:

1. On the www.myspace.com home page, click SignUp in the top-right corner (**FIGURE 3.1**).

   This takes you directly to the signup page (**FIGURE 3.2**).

2. Provide your email address, first and last name, date of birth, gender, country, and zip code.

   Your email address and last name won't appear in your public profile automatically, but your first name, age, and location will unless you delete them later. (We'll show you how.)

3. Create a unique password with six or more characters, containing at least one number or punctuation character.

4. Agree to comply with basic site-security protocols and the terms of the site by checking the appropriate check box.

5. Enter the characters displayed in the Verification box.

   You may have trouble deciphering the verification text, but if you get it wrong, MySpace will display a different one for you to try again.

6. Click the Sign Up button.

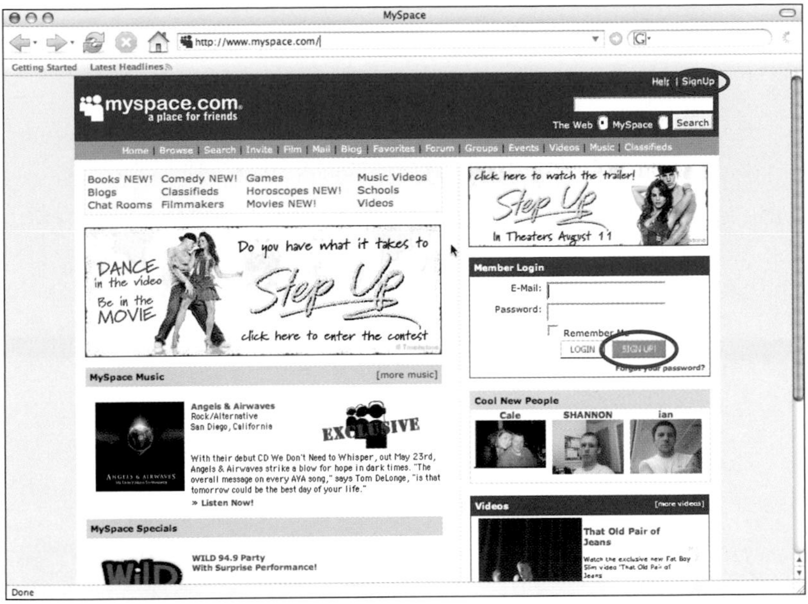

FIGURE 3.1 To sign up, click the orange button on the right side or click SignUp in the top-right corner.

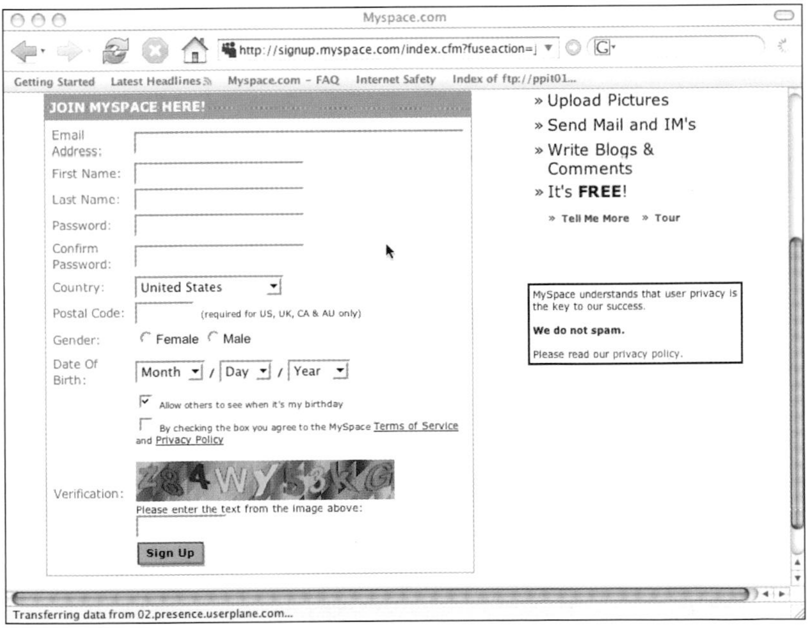

FIGURE 3.2 The signup page.

Parents may want to take a look at MySpace's terms of use and safety tips, and go over them with their kids. MySpace is getting more responsive to complaints about violations of these terms, including deleting the accounts of people under the minimum age of 14 and accounts that violate its terms.

Uploading a Photo

The next step is uploading a photo to your MySpace profile. Or you can choose to skip this step until later by selecting the Skip for Now link at the bottom of the page (**FIGURE 3.3**). See "Turning MySpace into YourSpace" later in this chapter if you want to upload your photo later.

FIGURE 3.3 Here, you can upload a photo or click Skip for Now to do it later.

If you have a good digital picture readily available on your computer, you can upload it this way:

1. Click Browse to navigate to the folder on your computer's hard drive where you store pictures.

2. Double-click the photo you want to use.

3. Click Upload.

It may take a minute or so for the photo to be uploaded from your hard drive to MySpace.

Note: See "Turning MySpace into YourSpace" later in this chapter for more about photos, including some safety warnings and instructions on changing your photo or adding a caption.

KEY PARENTING POINT

Be sure that you and your teen read the MySpace safety tips, and remind your child that any picture that gets posted can be seen and copied by anyone who has access to the profile. It can also be saved and passed around the Internet even after your child deletes it. Ask your teen how he or she would feel if the photos were seen by college admissions counselors, future employers, or Aunt Sophie.

Inviting Friends

Before you can view your new basic profile, you'll be asked to share your new page and invite your friends to MySpace (**FIGURE 3.4**). You can choose

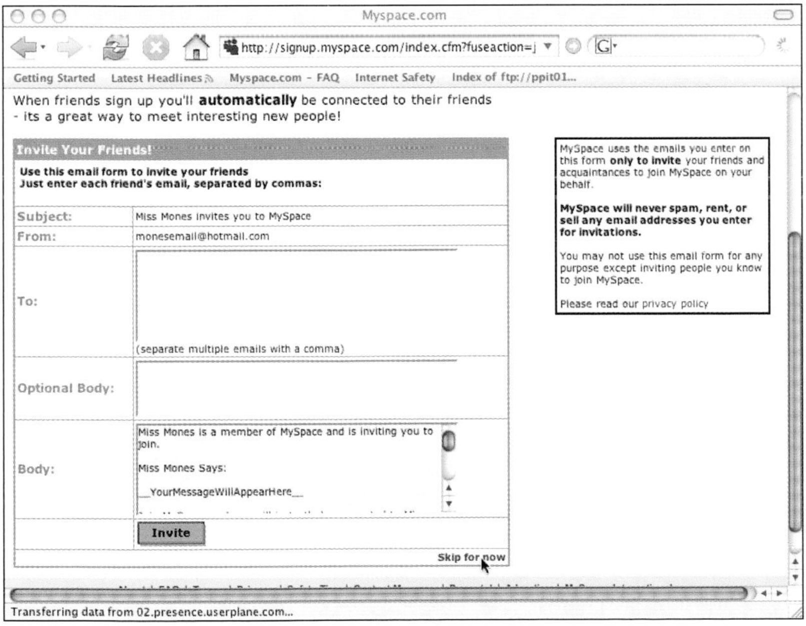

FIGURE 3.4 You can invite friends during setup or click Skip for Now to do it later.

to notify your contacts by following the address-input instructions or skip
this step until later.

The Hello Page

Congratulations—your new MySpace account is active! The Hello page
essentially is your MySpace home page and central site-navigation tool.
Your home page is unique, and it's different from MySpace's main home
page at www.myspace.com.

You can access your home page by clicking Home in the menu
near the top of any screen in MySpace. To get to the *site's* main home
page, click the MySpace.com link in the top corner of any screen
(**FIGURE 3.5**).

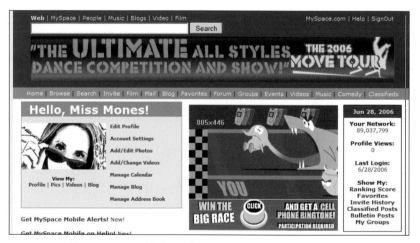

FIGURE 3.5 Your very own MySpace home page.

Every time you log in with your user name and password, you'll
be autodirected to your home page. Your home page is your
jumping-off point for editing or enhancing your profile. Only you
have access to this page. Though it looks a lot like what the public sees,
it's actually a little different. The URL of the page the public will see
is displayed in the box that says "Tell people about your MySpace"
(**FIGURE 3.6**).

```
                                                    ┌──────┐
                                                    │ Help │
            Pick your MySpace Name/URL!             └──────┘
                    Click Here

    ┌──────────────────────────────────────────────────┐
    │      Tell people about your MySpace [?]           │
    │                                                    │
    │                    My URL                          │
    │        http://www.myspace.com/84395566             │
    │                                                    │
    │                  My Blog URL                       │
    │        http://blog.myspace.com/84395566            │
    └──────────────────────────────────────────────────┘

            Make MySpace my Home Page
```

FIGURE 3.6 Here's where you can choose a URL that isn't a bunch of mind-numbing numbers.

Getting a Friendly MySpace URL

The web address (URL) in the "Tell people about your MySpace" area probably looks something like http://www.myspace.com/84395566. Unless your friends have good heads for numbers, none of them will remember that. Fortunately, just below that listing is a box that says "Pick your MySpace Name/URL!" If you click that box, you can replace those numbers with something people can remember. If your choice has already been used by another member, you'll get an error message and a chance to try a different word.

By the way, in case you were wondering, *URL* stands for *uniform resource locator*. Don't ya just love techie terms?

There actually is an upside and a downside to an all-numbers URL. If an address is harder to remember, it's also harder to find—whether the finder is a parent or someone with bad intentions. It's a good talking point for parents and kids.

Your MySpace home page has several features and tools, some of which we will highlight in this section and expand on in greater detail later in this chapter.

Up to this point, you've provided only basic profile information, so your home page looks pretty sparse. The steps in the following sections let you flesh out your profile by providing details.

KEY PARENTING POINT

For privacy and protection, especially if you log into MySpace on public or shared computers, we recommend that you and your kids follow certain practices when logging in and out. When signing in to MySpace (or any password-requiring site), make sure that the "Remember Me" box remains unchecked. When you're finished using MySpace, close out completely by clicking Sign Out in the top-right corner of any screen. We provide more information about passwords in Chapter 5.

MySpace: Subject to Change without Notice

As this book was going to press, the Hello box went through some changes. We think we caught it in time, but it reminded us that MySpace can change at any moment. It's not likely to change radically on any given day, but the company does tweak the interface now and then, which can affect how you use the service. If you come across a discrepancy between our instructions and what you see on the screen, don't blame us—in fact—don't blame anyone. That's the nature of the Web.

Also keep in mind that if something doesn't work right, it might not be your fault. It could be a bug, as we discovered when reviewing a couple of new features. That's a price we pay for living on the cutting edge. But we have good news—we guess: This book is set in stone, and until the next edition, it won't change.

Personalizing Your Profile

MySpace requires only basic information to create and maintain a user account. But as you cruise around the site, you'll notice that most users—especially teens—add a great deal of detail and personality. The more information they share, of course, the more information they're giving out to the general public, which is why in Chapter 5, we advise parents to remind teens to be very careful about the type of information they put out there.

To add to your profile, click the Edit Profile link in the blue box in the top-left corner of your home page (**FIGURE 3.7**).

FIGURE 3.7 Click the Edit Profile link.

The Profile Edit – Interests & Personality page appears (**FIGURE 3.8**). This is where you begin adding information about yourself. Other categories for adding information, such as Name, Basic Info, and Background & Lifestyle can be accessed using the tabs at the top of the page.

Note that you have full ownership of your profile and are free to answer questions and fill in boxes (or not), as you wish. If you don't feel comfortable answering certain questions, don't bother. When MySpace loads your profile, it will show only populated fields. Questions and categories left blank will be invisible. A few fields, however, will be filled in automatically.

In most cases, you have the option to delete or change the automatically populated fields. You can change your display name, for example (by default, it's your first name), or remove or change the name of your town. You can

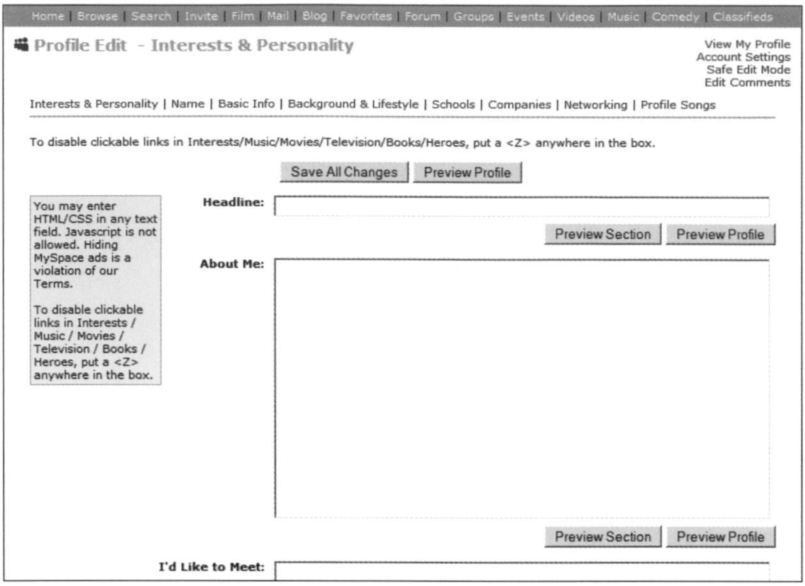

FIGURE 3.8 The Profile Edit page, where you can write anything about yourself in the boxes beside the headings.

even change your gender (well, what you say is your gender) and your date of birth. See the section "Adding a display name" for details on how to do this.

Adding Interests and Personality Details

The Profile Edit - Interests & Personality page (Figure 3.8) has text boxes that allow creative expression, including, from some teens, information that probably shouldn't be there. You can leave any of these boxes blank, or you can type anything you want the public to see. As we explain in Chapter 7, some people even add HTML to some of these boxes to enhance (or mess up) their pages.

Note: Don't worry too much about HTML; you don't have to use it, and even if you do decide to use it, you don't have to know much about it, as we'll explain in Chapter 7.

Your browser will be directed to this page after you've set up your account. If you want to alter this page later, you can access it by clicking the Edit Profile link in the Hello box on your home page.

You can add anything from short 'n' sweet comments to lengthy descriptions and details:

- **Headline.** The headline is a short, simple statement or personal handle.

- **About Me.** This section is for your personal bio or statement—a verbal snapshot of who you are. Content here varies greatly, from funny, interesting, and succinct to obnoxiously verbose to pure, unintelligible slang.

- **I'd Like to Meet.** You can list specific people you'd like to meet (celebrities, historic figures, athletes), groups (such as a band or team), or general types of people.

- **Interests.** Here, you present information about what makes you tick, such as hobbies, interests, activities, and joys (**FIGURE 3.9**).

- **Music.** Music has its own category because it's such a big personality piece. You can learn a lot about people based on their musical tastes, and MySpace users have the option to express and define themselves by providing detail about their musical likes and dislikes.

- **Movies, Television, and Books.** MySpace users can elaborate further on their entertainment likes and dislikes in these sections.

- **Heroes.** Typically, users put the name of a real or fictional person here, but many people skip this question.

Keeping It Safe

It's important for kids to know that they don't have to answer all the questions that appear on the Profile Edit pages, given the personal nature of these details. Although 22-year-old adults might feel comfortable disclosing their sexual preferences, drinking/smoking preferences, or where they went to school, such details may be unnecessary, inappropriate, or even unsafe for a teenager. MySpace has restrictions on inappropriate language and images. Threatening, violent, or explicit content is unacceptable, and MySpace will delete accounts it discovers that are in violation of these restrictions. For better or worse, however, most of the millions of profiles are unregulated, and users are able to express themselves freely.

Miss Mones's Interests	
General	Reading, writing, music, travel, soccer, yoga/pilates, cooking, long outdoor walks, dancing, biking, films, good food and drink, great company/conversation...hanging out with friends, kitties, copyediting, German, comedy, and Trader Joes.
Music	Styles: Alt./Rock, Lounge, Trip-Hop/Acid Jazz, 80's. Bands/Artists: U2, Tori Amos, Hooverphonic, Beck, Radiohead, Coldplay, Massive Attack, Gomez, The Shins, Interpol, The Postal Service, Franz Ferdinand, Miles End, lounge music. New likes: The Lovemakers, The Killers, Death Cab for Cutie, Pinback. Old faves: Beatles, Led Zepplin, Depeche Mode, Garbage, Cranberries, The Cure.
Movies	The Princess Bride and many more!
Television	24, Grey's Anatomy, Sex and the City, The Family Guy, The Simpsons
Books	Right now I'm reading The Beach by Alex Garland.
Heroes	Bono

FIGURE 3.9 The interests page is how you represent yourself online.

Adding a Display Name

MySpace recommends you create a "display name" for your profile (elsewhere known as a screenname). That's your MySpace moniker and can be anything you want—your first name, nickname, or any other label:

1. At the top of the Profile Edit–Interests & Personality page, click the Name link.

   The Profile Edit - Name page appears. On this page, you're likely to see the name you entered when you signed up.

2. Leave the display name as it is, or type a different one (**FIGURE 3.10**).

3. Click Save Changes.

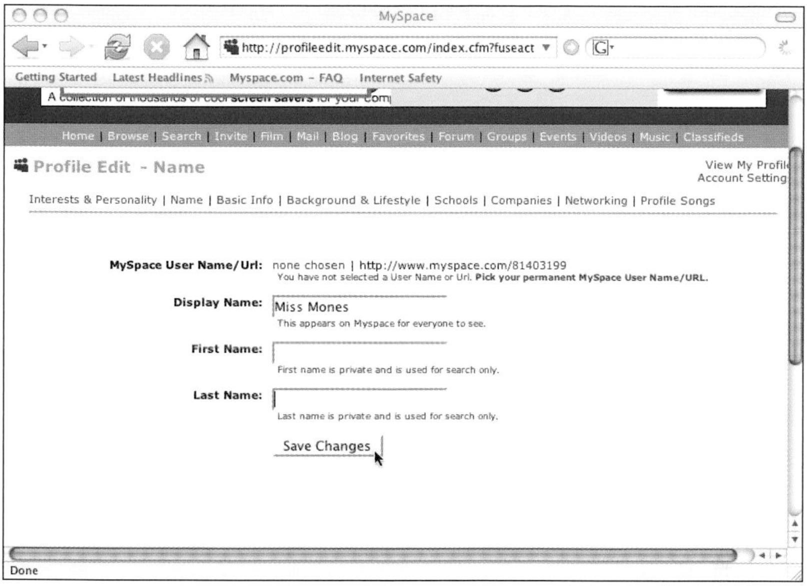

FIGURE 3.10 Your display or screen name: how everybody identifies you on MySpace.

Your display name won't show up in your profile but will be stored in the MySpace database, allowing other users who know your name to search for you. For complete anonymity, you can opt to fill in only the display name and delete your last name if it's there by default. This makes it more difficult for friends to find you on MySpace, which is something many teenagers want to avoid.

KEY PARENTING POINT

We recommend that all users, teens and adults, consider using nicknames and other names for privacy—and at the very least not to use last names. It's also a good idea, especially for teens, to avoid nicknames that are sexually suggestive.

Adding Background and Lifestyle Details

To access this page, click the Background *&* Lifestyle link at the top of any of the Profile Edit pages.

The majority of questions on this page are purely optional; again, parents can remind their kids that they don't need to answer all the questions. Users can reveal more information about themselves by checking applicable selections for:

- Marital status (not optional)
- Sexual orientation (see below)
- Hometown
- Religion
- Smoker
- Drinker
- Children
- Education
- Income

KEY PARENTING POINT

A lot of people use MySpace and other social networks to seek out a potential romantic interest or just to flirt—which, we suppose, is why MySpace asks about sexual orientation. But before teens check this box and provide more detail, have them consider the consequences. Ask whether it's really necessary to give out this information. We suspect that most teens would answer "yes," but it's this type of information that a potential predator will look at.

The option that concerns us the most is "not sure," because a predator could interpret that comment as coming from a someone who is insecure about his or her sexuality. We feel that the default option, "no answer," is a safer choice.

Including School Information

Almost all kids list the name of their school. We prefer that kids not give out that information, because it does help predators locate them. Actually, though, this cat is already out of the bag. The whole point of social networking is to help people find one another—ideally, people they know from the real world.

Kids' lives revolve around school, and given the culture of MySpace, there's almost no way to persuade most teens not to reveal their school name, because it helps them find classmates. This, by itself, is one of the positive and safe aspects of the service. Assuming that teens do give out their school name, the key is to avoid giving out too much other information, as we discuss throughout this book.

But this advice isn't just for kids. In addition to current school, users can list former schools on the Profile Edit – Schools page, along with lots of optional information that can help fellow alums find one another.

To access the Schools page, click the Schools link at the top of any Profile Edit page.

Adding Employer Information

Though this section applies mainly to adults, it can affect teens with part-time or summer jobs as well. Users can include former and current employers in their profile. This can provide opportunities to network and socialize with co-workers, but it also makes it easier for an employer to find your profile. There have been cases in which employees have been fired (and students disciplined) as a result of postings that the employer or school considered to be inappropriate, illegal, or in violation of policy. Parents can help kids remember that.

To access this page, click the Companies link at the top of any Profile Edit page.

Listing Areas of Interest for Networking

MySpace is a social network that many people use to reach out to others with similar interests. These interests can be business-related, political, artistic, or purely social. There are other places in the service (including groups) where you can find like-minded people, but by specifying your networking interests, you can make it easier for people with similar interests to find you.

You can also select networking categories in specific fields and industries to add to your profile.

If you display your networking interests in your profile, other writers, dancers, or marketing people on MySpace can find you when they search for people with a specific affiliation.

To access the page, click the Networking link at the top of any Profile Edit page.

After you've added all the details about yourself to your profile, click the View My Profile link in the top-right corner of the page to preview your profile (**FIGURE 3.11**).

FIGURE 3.11 The results at last! Now you can review your profile.

TIP

It's also a good idea to view your home page as others will see it, using the public URL, and then change anything you feel is inappropriate, ugly, or just plain dumb (not that parents ever do dumb things).

Setting Privacy Options

MySpace gives you some control of how other people can find you, contact you, and view or comment on your profile. In most cases, MySpace sets the default privacy settings to the least private options (except for people who are 14 or 15 years old, whose accounts can be viewed by friends only or anyone younger than 18 on MySpace).

As this book was going to press, MySpace announced that all MySpace users have the option of making their profiles private. Prior to this announcement, private profiles were available only to 14 and 15 year olds. As of this writing, the default settings for users who register as being 16 or older are likely to remain public, so it's still a good idea to customize the privacy settings to a level that's comfortable for you or your teen.

MySpace Privacy: A Moving Target

MySpace changed its privacy options in late June 2006, just as this book went to press. When we learned of the news, we contacted a company official, who stated the obvious: "These types of changes can happen at any time, as our site is a work in progress." She added, "This is the problem with putting things down in print about the Internet--change happens so very fast."

It appears MySpace changed its privacy options in two significant ways. First, all users—not just 14 and 15 year olds—have the option to make their profiles private. Second, new restrictions have been imposed on how adults can contact users under 16. Under the new rules, MySpace users who are 18 or older can no longer send a request to be on the friends list of a 14 or 15 year old unless the adult already knows the teen's full name or email address.

Of course, all of these changes to MySpace's privacy options are based on "the honor system." Until reliable age verification technology is developed and implemented, a child under 16 can register as being older, and an adult can pose as a teenager.

KEY PARENTING POINT

Setting a young person's profile so that it can be read by anyone younger than 18 on MySpace hides the profile from only those people who say they're 18 or older. Because there is no age-verification process, it's possible for adults to say they're under 18 and still view these profiles. Also, even a private profile can be searched. The full profile won't be displayed, but some basic information can be viewed.

To view or make changes to your privacy settings, follow these steps:

1. On your MySpace home page, click the Account Settings link (**FIGURE 3.12**).

FIGURE 3.12 Click Account Settings to display your privacy options.

2. Scroll down to Privacy Settings, and select Change Settings.
3. To change certain settings, simply check the applicable check boxes and then click Change Settings (**FIGURE 3.13**).

Choices include:

- **Require Email or Last Name to Add Me As a Friend.** This setting gives you a little more privacy by preventing people from adding you as

My Privacy Settings	
☐	Require email or last name to add me as a friend
☐	Approve Comments before Posting
☐	Hide Online Now
☑	Show My Birthday to my Friends ☝
☐	No Pic Forwarding
☐	Friend Only Blog Comments
☐	Block Friend Request From Bands
☐	Friend Only Group Invites
☐	Disable Band Songs From Automatically Starting
Who Can View My Full Profile	
○	My Friends Only
⊙	Public

Change Settings   Cancel

FIGURE 3.13 Select the privacy options you want.

a friend unless they know your email address or last name. To add you, they have to know at least a little bit about you.

- **Approve Comments Before Posting.** By default, any of your MySpace friends can post comments to your profile page. Such comments can be embarrassing or could violate your privacy. Although you can delete them later, the comments will stay there until you do. It's a smart idea to check this check box, because it gives you the power to approve comments before they're posted. The only downside is that friends who post comments have to wait a while before the world can see them. But others can't post malicious or just stupid comments to your page.

- **Hide Online Now.** By default, other MySpace users can tell whether you're online. That can be handy if they want to send you an instant message, but you may not want to tell the world that you or your kids are sitting at a computer using MySpace at this very moment (it's a pretty good clue that you're home, which you may not want others to know). Selecting this check box hides that display.

- **Show My Birthday to My Friends.** This option (checked by default) tells your friends that it's time to send you a gift or at least a "Happy birthday" greeting. It's relatively safe, but birthdays are one of many pieces of information that identity thieves use.

- **No Pic Forwarding.** If you turn this option off, you're preventing other users from emailing your photo to any MySpace user they choose. Not allowing pic forwarding gives you only a little more control of your picture—people with a little more tech know-how can still copy your photo and paste it wherever they want. But even a little bit of control helps.

- **Friend Only Blog Comments.** By default, anyone can post to your blog. This option limits blog postings to friends only. As we discuss in "Blogging" in Chapter 4, a blog is separate from your basic profile; many MySpace users don't use blogs.

- **Block Friend Request from Bands.** As we said earlier, music is the soul of MySpace, and it's set up for bands and fans to connect, which is why a lot of people like to include bands as their "friends." The downside, however, is that you could get unwanted email from bands you don't want to hear from, so checking this option means that bands can't send you requests to be among your friends. Even if you block these requests, you can still initiate contact with bands and add them as your friends.

- **Friend Only Group Invites.** MySpace groups enable people to invite others to join them to discuss a variety of topics. But you may get more invitations than you bargained for, so when you choose this option, you get invitations only from your friends.

- **Disable Band Songs from Automatically Starting.** This setting is more for your sanity and peace of mind than for your privacy. As you surf around MySpace, you'll hear a lot of music, whether you want to or not. Sometimes, it can be distracting. So by checking this option, you won't hear the music.

When kids are registered with MySpace as being 16 years old or older, the Who Can View My Full Profile section at the bottom of the privacy settings window provides two options:

- **My Friends Only.** Only the people on a person's friends list can view the profile.

- **Public.** The profile can be viewed by anyone. This is the default option, so it has to be changed if you or your teen want more control.

When kids are registered with MySpace as being 14 or 15 years old, the Who Can View My Full Profile section at the bottom of the privacy settings window provides a different set of options (**FIGURE 3.14**):

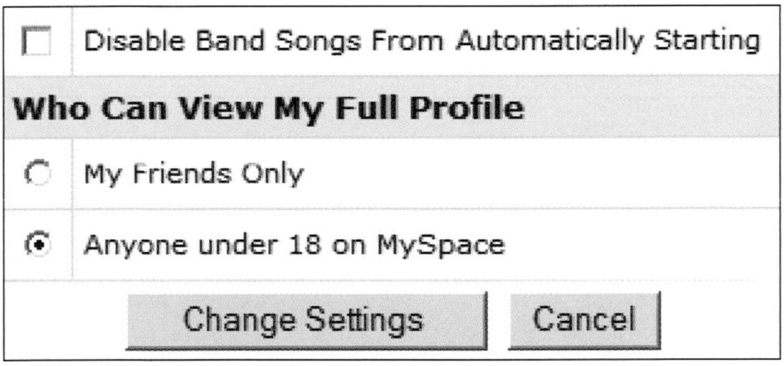

FIGURE 3.14 These extra privacy options are only for people who register as being 14 or 15 years old.

- **My Friends Only.** Only the people on a person's friends list can view the profile.

- **Anyone Under 18 on MySpace.** Only MySpace users who say they are 18 years old or younger can view the profile. This is the default option.

Note: What you see onscreen may look different from Figure 3.14, since MySpace was just announcing these changes as this book went to press. Keep in mind that the settings could change further as MySpace rolls out additional privacy settings.

Adjusting Other Account Settings

In addition to privacy settings, MySpace has extensive account settings that let you customize your account and profile. You can change your email address. You can prevent MySpace from sending notices to your regular email account (not your MySpace account).

Just click any category you want to explore or change in your Hello box, including Privacy Settings (see the preceding section), IM Privacy Settings, Mobile Settings, Group Settings, Calendar Settings, Blocked Users, Profile Views, Profile Settings, Music Settings, and Away Messages.

When you click any of these categories, you'll see an explanation of what it does and how you can change it (**FIGURE 3.15**).

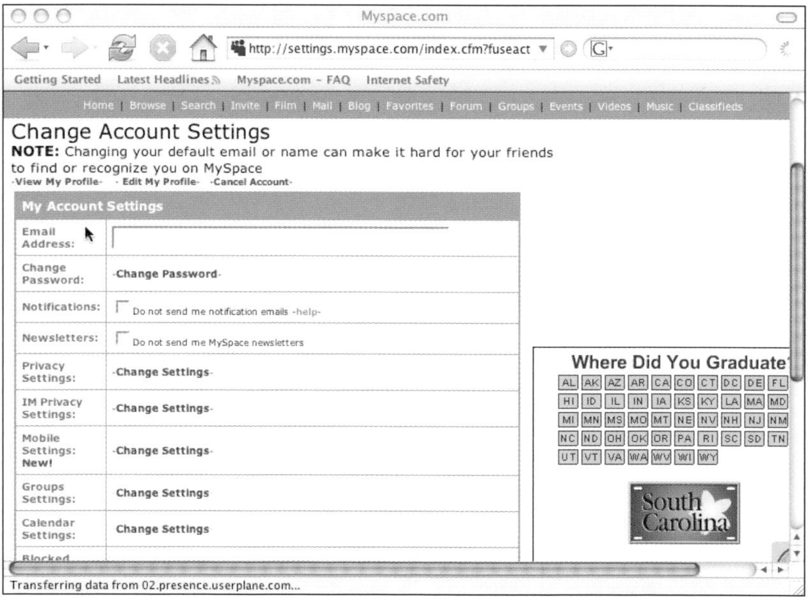

FIGURE 3.15 Click the text in red to change settings in a category.

Making adjustments or changing settings in all these categories is a lot like the profile-management process we walked you through earlier in this chapter. You may notice an option called Mobile Settings, however. This option determines how users can access MySpace with their cell phones.

To make any adjustments, follow these steps:

1. On your MySpace home page, click the Account Settings link in your Hello box (see Figure 3.5).

2. Explore your options, view the help messages MySpace provides with them, and make any appropriate changes.

The rest of this section gives you specifics on some settings of particular interest to parents of MySpace users.

Blocking Users

The Blocked Users feature lets you view and unblock the users or groups that were blocked previously. (This is not the area where you can initially block a user. To do that, you must visit that user's profile and click Block User in the Contacting section just beneath the profile photo.)

The Block User feature is sort of a cross between a spam filter and a digital restraining order. Blocked users can still view your profile, but they cannot send you a message or communicate with you.

KEY PARENTING POINT

Some users "hack" their profile to obscure or deemphasize this box, making it hard to find the block feature. For more details about hacks and advanced profile design, see Chapter 7.

Profile Settings

These settings give you control of some of the information others can see in your profile, as well as whether they can use HTML in comments that appear in your profile.

We talk more about HTML in Chapter 7, but in short, HTML is simple computer code that gives people a great deal of control not only of how things look in a profile, but also of how they act (flashing text, special fonts, sounds, graphics, and so on).

Poorly written HTML can cause MySpace and your browser to crash and can even crash your computer or—in theory—violate your privacy. By default (at this writing), MySpace lets users post HTML comments on your page. That can make your page look very cool, but it can also cause problems. Disabling the ability for others to add HTML to your page can prevent these types of problems.

To change the HTML Comments option, follow these steps:

1. Click Change Settings.

2. If you want your friends and other MySpace users to know what groups you are interested in, check the Display Groups I Belong To check box (**FIGURE 3.16**).

    Each name of a MySpace group that you belong to will be displayed as a text link in the My Groups section of your profile.

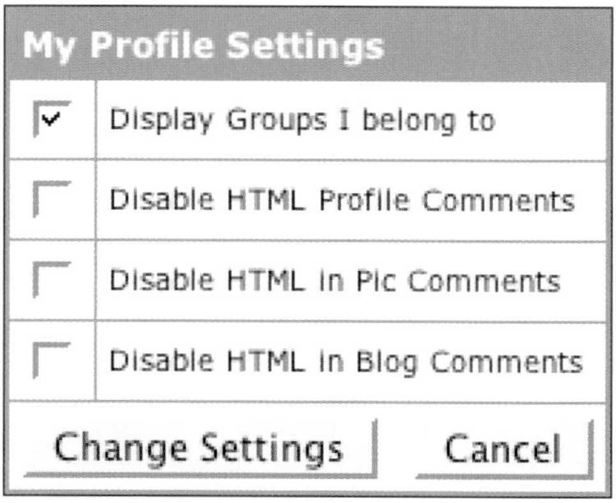

FIGURE 3.16 Displaying your groups shows people more about your interests and affiliations.

3. If you want to prevent people from posting images in the comments section of your profile, check Disable HTML Profile Comments.

4. When you finish making your selections, click the Change Settings button.

Because HTML is a programming language, it's possible to use it to do a lot. This includes linking to other Web sites and embedding in MySpace pages images and video that are actually stored on other sites—in other words, photos and clips that may violate MySpace's rules and harm users' computers or jeopardize their privacy, despite the fact that MySpace takes steps to minimize these risks. Urge your kids to be very careful about using HTML, including code that they paste in from other sites. For more information about HTML, see Chapter 7.

Music Settings

These settings can help you control the way the music player works when people access your profile or when you access other people's profiles.

Music is an integral part of kids' identity and culture, which is why a lot of kids not only use it in their profiles, but also configure it to play automatically when people go there. Still, sometimes silence really is golden, which is why MySpace gives users to the option of disabling music from starting automatically when you visit other people's profiles and when they visit yours.

To view or change the music settings, follow these steps:

1. Click Change Settings.
2. To prevent the music player from playing when people view your profile, check Disable My Player from Automatically Starting.

TIP

If visitors want to hear the music, they can start it manually by clicking the play button in the music player.

3. To prevent music from playing automatically as you browse other people's profiles, check Disable Band Songs from Automatically Starting.
4. Click the Change Settings button to save your changes.

In "Turning MySpace into YourSpace," later in this chapter, we'll tell you how to add music to your profile.

Away Message

If you plan to be away from your computer or just off MySpace for a while (which we think is a good idea from time to time!), you can display an away message that people will get when they send you a message. By default, there is no such message in MySpace, but you can click on Edit Away Message in Account Settings to create one (**FIGURE 3.17**). Make sure that you save your message when you finish writing it.

KEY PARENTING POINT

Kids can get very creative with their away messages, which can be fun, but caution your teens not to use the away message to reveal anything inappropriate, including where they plan to be while away from the computer.

FIGURE 3.17 Here's where you explain where you're off to.

Turning MySpace Into YourSpace

As you navigate MySpace and check out profiles, you'll notice that the look and feel varies tremendously from user to user. Some people have profiles with a personalized description, unique photos, and perhaps a little extra here and there; others have decked out their pages with crazy fonts, glitzy wallpaper, music, and video graphics (**FIGURE 3.18**). You don't have to do any of this fancy customizing, but if you are curious about how it's done, check out Chapter 7.

FIGURE 3.18 One of the more souped-up profiles we've seen.

Photos

People are visual creatures, so naturally, they want to look at pictures. The popular MySpace photo feature lets you upload up to eight digital photos or images (including your profile image) to your profile. Photos let you share more about yourself and your life, including friends, family members, and pets.

You can upload virtually any image: artwork, graphics, illustrations, cartoons, pictures, and other images. All photos must be in .gif or .jpg format and no larger than 600 KB.

MySpace users often experiment and add a creative touch to their profiles by using popular or unique images in their profiles rather than traditional photographs or portraits. This can provide added privacy protection, too, but make sure that you and your kids know not to violate MySpace rules and federal law by posting copyrighted images without permission.

MySpace also prohibits photos that "contain nudity, violent or offensive material." Warn your kids that MySpace will delete their accounts if it catches them violating these terms.

Company policy and basic courtesy also prohibit uploading images of other people without their permission.

KEY PARENTING POINT

If you or your child come across photos that you believe violate these policies, you can report them to MySpace by clicking the Report This Image link below each photo you see in people's profiles. In Chapter 5, we talk more about photos and how to identify and report child pornography.

Sometimes, images or videos are actually stored on another site (as we mentioned in our discussion of HTML earlier in this chapter); they're not on MySpace at all. But because MySpace lets users add HTML to their profiles, users can add links to media at sites like Photobucket.com and YouTube.com.

Note: MySpace says it's negotiating with some of these sites to police the storage of media files that violate its terms, but that's a tall order, because media-storage and media-sharing sites are multiplying rapidly on Web 2.0.

If you didn't upload a photo when you created your MySpace account, you can always do it now.

To upload a photo, follow these steps:

1. Click the Add/Edit Photos link in the Hello box on your home page (**FIGURE 3.19**).

FIGURE 3.19 The Add/Edit Photos option.

2. Click Browse, which lets you navigate to the folder on your computer's hard drive where you store pictures.

3. Double-click the photo you want to use.

4. Click Upload.

    It may take a minute or so for the photo to be uploaded from your hard drive to MySpace.

You can opt to include a caption with the photo. You can do that from the same screen where you uploaded the photo, or you can do it later by clicking the Add/Edit Photos link on your home page.

To add a caption, follow these steps:

1. Scroll down to the bottom of the Upload Your Photo page where your photo appears, and click Add Caption below the photo.

2. Write your caption in the text box.

3. Click Update Caption.

    A Confirm Caption screen displays.

4. If you're satisfied with the caption, click Post Caption; otherwise, click the Back button, and make changes.

KEY PARENTING POINT

Although MySpace prohibits nude photos, it doesn't necessarily censor photos that could be suggestive or otherwise inappropriate. Teens may need reminding that their photos can have an impact on how people perceive those who are depicted in them, whether it's themselves, their friends, or family members (some parents have been dismayed to find unflattering pictures of themselves in their kids' profiles). Photos can also easily be copied and pasted into others' Web pages and sent around via email. So once the photos are posted, their owners have little control over them. Ideally, it's best that the photos at least not clearly identify the young people in them, though that may be a tough sell, considering the millions of photos on the service that do just that.

Adding Music to Your Profile

A lot of kids display their "music personality" by uploading a song to play automatically when people visit their profile and changing it often. Unlike some services, MySpace allows users to upload songs only from bands that are already on the service. You can't upload MP3 or iTunes files from your own collection. This is MySpace's way of promoting its member bands and trying to make sure that users don't upload copyrighted music without permission.

To upload a profile song, follow these steps:

1. In your Hello box, click the Edit Profile link.

2. Click the Profile Songs link (**FIGURE 3.20**).
   The Add a Song to Your Profile page displays.

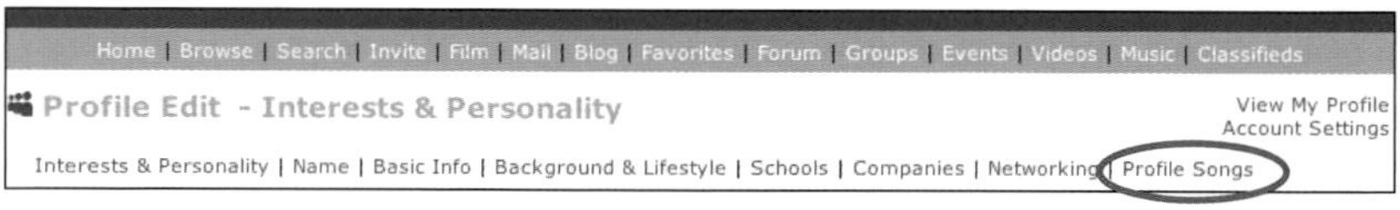

FIGURE 3.20 Profile songs is the last Profile Edit option on the right.

3. To start searching for a song, click Find a Band in MySpace Music (**FIGURE 3.21**).

4. Enter the band name in the keyword search box, and click Search.
   At least one band profile appears.

FIGURE 3.21 Browse for a tune by clicking the blue text.

5. Select the appropriate profile by clicking the band's name (**FIGURE 3.22**).
   A song most likely will start playing automatically.

6. Choose the song that's playing or another song, and click Add.
   A confirmation page appears, asking whether you're sure you
   want to add the song to your profile.

7. Click the Add Song to Profile button (**FIGURE 3.23**).
   A final band-upload confirmation screen appears (**FIGURE 3.24**).

Voilà! You've added tunes to your MySpace profile.

To remove a son from your profile, follow these steps:

1. Complete steps 1 and 2 in the preceding list.

2. Click Remove next to the song and artist you want to remove.

Adding Video to Your Profile

Similar to MySpace Music, the Videos feature lets users share their favorite
clips and shorts directly in their profiles. You can see these videos playing

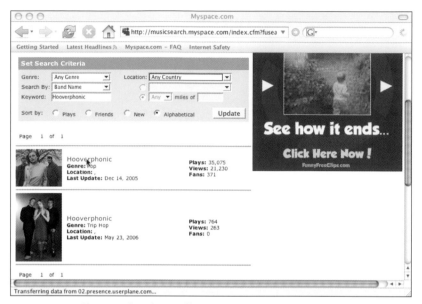

FIGURE 3.22 Choose a band's profile to check out its songs.

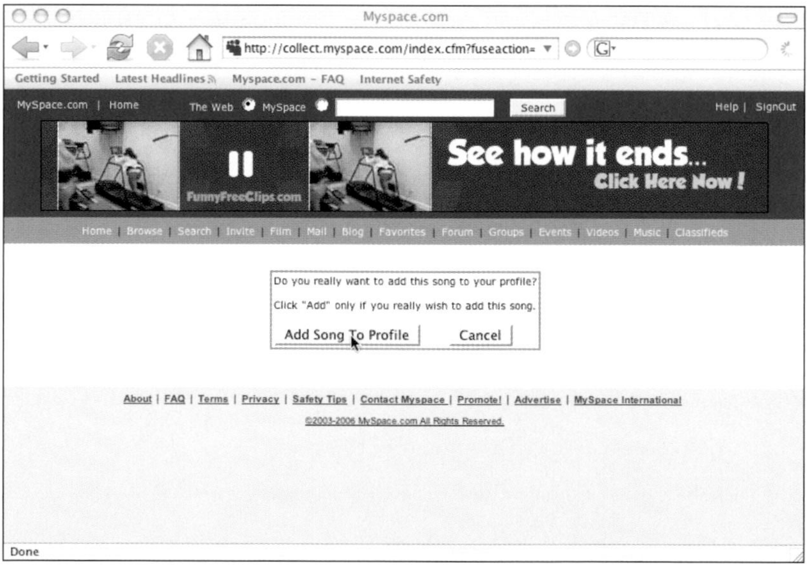

FIGURE 3.23 Choose a song and then add it to your profile.

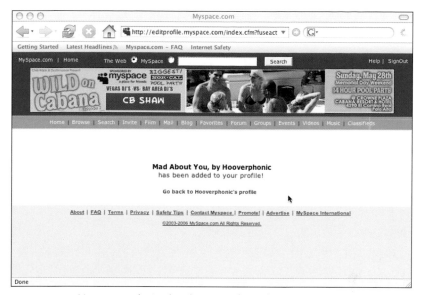

FIGURE 3.24 Your tune choice has been confirmed.

when you visit profiles, and sometimes, you can see several videos at the same time, which can be a real challenge for grownup eyes. Still, these videos are very important to the way kids present themselves, and they're a very popular feature on the service.

It's also possible to upload home videos to a home page. Kids are increasingly using camcorders or even video-enabled cell phones to shoot their own video and then uploading it to MySpace and other video sharing services. Many of the kid-generated videos we've seen are terrific, and some are very funny. (If you really want to delve into this, check out YouTube.com and Grouper.com, two social-networking sites that specialize in video.)

KEY PARENTING POINT

Naturally, parents are going to worry about their kids viewing and, especially, posting inappropriate videos. As with photos, MySpace has a strict antiporn policy and actually checks out user-supplied videos before they're posted to make sure that they don't violate the rules. That, however, is no guarantee that kids won't post homemade videos that jeopardize their own privacy, so parents still need to be on the alert. And as with all media these days, your idea of what's OK might not necessarily be the same as the MySpace policy. That's why parents—not the government or corporations—are the ultimate arbiters for their own kids.

We suspect that most parents aren't going to be uploading their own video, but if you want to know how it's done, check out Chapter 7.

Calendars

MySpace has an easy-to-use calendar to help you track your schedule or your family's schedule. Kids can use it to help coordinate their lives and share their calendars with their friends.

One nice family-friendly feature we really like is the ability to configure the calendar to send you a reminder via your MySpace mail, your "external" (regular email account) mail, or both. That way, you won't forget an appointment, a friend's birthday, or the date of your child's parent–teacher conference, and maybe your kids will even use it to remind themselves of important after-school practices and lessons.

You create your calendar by clicking the Manage Calendar link in the blue box on your home page, adjacent to your picture. To enter an event, click the time when the event will start, and fill out the form just as you would any computer-based calendar.

The Calendar Sharing option lets you control who can view your calendar. Select the appropriate choice from the Calendar Sharing drop-down menu (**FIGURE 3.25**). Your choices are Share with Friends (the default), Disabled (for maximum privacy), and Share with Everyone (if you want the world to know what you're doing and when).

KEY PARENTING POINT

By default, your calendar is shared with your friends, but you can disable sharing or decide to share your calendar with everyone. As you've probably guessed, the latter option generally is a bad idea, especially for teens, because it lets anyone know what they're doing and when they're doing it.

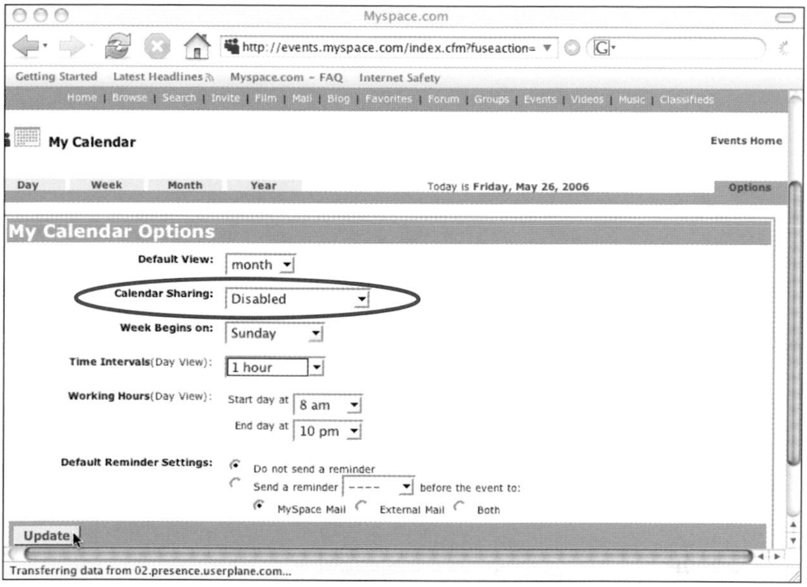

FIGURE 3.25 Disabling sharing is definitely the safest option.

Canceling an Account

If you want to terminate your MySpace account, here's how:

1. Log into MySpace, and click the Account Settings link on your MySpace home page.

2. On your Account Settings page, click the Cancel Account link in red at the top of the page (see Figure 3.14).

3. On the Cancel MySpace Account page, click the Cancel My Account button (**FIGURE 3.26**).

   A confirmation email message will be sent to the email account you used to create your MySpace account (**FIGURE 3.27**).

4. Locate the email message that was sent to you, and follow the instructions in that email to delete your account.

FIGURE 3.26 Click the red "Cancel My Account" button in the Confirm Cancel Account box.

FIGURE 3.27 The address you used to sign up on MySpace is the one MySpace will send your cancellation instructions to. If the address that was used wasn't real, see the sidebar "Canceling Your Child's Account" in Chapter 6.

TIP

MySpace warns you, "Canceling your MySpace account will permanently remove all of your profile information from MySpace, including your photographs, comments, journals, and your personal network of friends. This information cannot be restored." Users can create a new account at any time, but may have to use a different email address (not a problem, when free email accounts can be established at Hotmail, Yahoo!, etc. at any time). Parents considering canceling kids' accounts might encounter strong reactions, given the social and time investments that go into these profiles.

We've covered the basics of setting up and managing a profile, which is all you really need to get started. But turn the page. In Chapter 4, we cover the all-important topic of how people are using MySpace to manage their social lives, with plenty more "hands-on" tips on how kids and adults can use this service.

.

CHAPTER 4

Managing the Social Stuff

MYSPACE'S TAGLINE IS "a place for friends," and true to its word, the site provides numerous tools for socializing and managing a network of friends.

This chapter builds on basic account management you learned about in Chapter 3, providing a step-by-step exploration of the tools and communities on MySpace that help young users manage the online part of their busy social lives. By getting a basic sense of how this management is done, we hope you will feel less daunted and more free to engage in your child's involvement with MySpace. Who knows? You might find it helps you manage your own online social life— except that you'll have to get your whole book club to join MySpace too!

Making and Managing Friends

We feel compelled to make a distinction between the friends you make on MySpace and the friends you actually know in the real world. As it turns out, most of the teens we've spoken with tell us that they use the service mainly to communicate with kids they know from school or other real-world venues; to communicate with bands; or, in some cases, to communicate with people who have common interests in sports, games, politics, and other activities.

MySpace does have features that let you respond to and seek out people you meet through the service, of course. We urge that teens use these features cautiously, if at all. This is especially important for young people who, as we discussed in Chapter 2, sometimes use social-networking sites to collect friends, treating the service as a sort of popularity contest. Obviously, they can be more vulnerable to contacts from strangers who want to become their "friends."

MySpace recently made it more difficult for adults to view the full profiles of 14- and 15-year-old users and to contact those users, but the additional protection depends on people being honest about their ages, as we mentioned in Chapter 3. So it's still possible that your kids will hear from strangers who want to be their friend.

Savvy teen users tell us that they never add such people to their friends lists without first checking out the profiles to be sure that there is a real connection, such as a person they know from school or elsewhere who has genuine shared interests, or at least a friend of a friend. We'll have a lot more to say about social-networking safety in the next chapter.

Adding Friends

Even if you have a public profile, there are certain privileges that are available only to people you designate as "friends." For example, only friends can post on your profile, comment on your picture or see certain information. If your profile is private, it's off-limits to all but your friends. That's

why, on MySpace as in life, it's important to remind your kids to choose
their friends carefully.

To add a friend who isn't a MySpace user:

1. Send an invitation by clicking the Invite link on the blue navigation
    bar to the top of any page (**FIGURE 4.1**).

FIGURE 4.1 To invite a friend, click Invite in the blue navigation bar at the top
of any MySpace page.

2. Enter your friend's email address, and type a message into the box
    below it (**FIGURE 4.2**).

FIGURE 4.2 Type the friends' email addresses (separated by commas) in the
To text box.

On the right side of the Invite page are options for importing contact
lists from your Yahoo!, Gmail, Hotmail, or AOL account. We suggest you
think carefully before doing this, however. If you do import one, MySpace,
by default, will send an invitation to everyone in your address book for
that account, unless you uncheck that person's name.

We think you're better off making a list of the friends you want to invite (and "checking it twice"), and then entering the email addresses one at a time.

To add friends or request a friend who is already on MySpace:

1. On the person's profile page, click the Add to Friends link in the Contacting box (**FIGURE 4.3**).

FIGURE 4.3 Click Add to Friends in the Contacting box on the left side of the profile page.

2. MySpace will ask if you really want to add the person. If so, click the Add to Friends button (**FIGURE 4.4**).

FIGURE 4.4 Click Add to Friends to confirm you really want to add that person to your friends list.

The person you're trying to add will get a "New Friend Request Message" (see the next section, "Accepting or Denying Friend Requests") and will have the option to Approve, Deny or Send you a message. If you're approved, you will show up on that person's friends list, and he or she will show up on yours.

Accepting or Denying Friend Requests

If you receive a new friend request, you'll receive notification in the My Mail section of your home page. You'll also be notified in your non–MySpace personal email account (the one you used to sign up with MySpace) if you chose in Account Settings to receive those external notifications (see "Adjusting Other Account Settings" in Chapter 3).

Friend requests, like all other notifications (Comments, Blogs, and Event Invites), are hard to miss. As soon as you log into MySpace, a little envelope and New Friend Requests! message appears in blue at the top of the My Mail area on your home page (**FIGURE 4.5**).

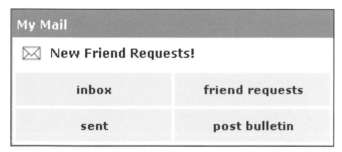

FIGURE 4.5 You've got a New Friend Request!

It is common to receive MySpace friend requests from people you know, as well as from complete strangers (unless you have a private profile). All requests are pending and remain so for a month. During that time, a user can view and explore the requester's profile, and has the choice to accept the request, deny the request, or contact the requester via MySpace mail. If you choose to do nothing, the request will disappear from your inbox in 30 days, and you will not be added to the person's friends list.

To accept or deny a friend request, follow these steps:

1. In the My Mail section of your home page, click the blue New Friend Requests! Link (see Figure 4.4).

    The Friend Request Manager page displays.

2. Click Approve to add the requester to your friends list, or click Deny to decline, in which case the request will be deleted from your inbox (**FIGURE 4.6**).

FIGURE 4.6 Approve or deny friend requests from this screen.

Inviters don't get any kind of notification when their requests have been denied (although they probably will figure it out when they don't end up being added to your friends list).

KEY PARENTING POINT

Don't forget: Remind your kids to be very cautious before accepting a request from someone they don't know in the real world—or at least register your concern, because they've probably heard it before. Even when people have very cool profiles and seem to be the type of people you'd like to get to know, that doesn't mean they are who they say they are. There have been numerous cases of people making up very convincing profiles that are totally fake.

We recommend that teens (and adults, too) use MySpace to hang out with people whom they truly know are who they say they are. A very good rule—especially for social networkers who are younger teens—is that their parents should also know everyone on their children's friends list—just as we'd want to know who they're hanging out with in person.

MySpace Doesn't Always Look or Act Like We Say It Will

MySpace may not always behave or look exactly the way we describe in this chapter. There are two reasons for this. One, of course, is that MySpace changes things; that's the nature of the Web. But the more likely reason—especially when you're visiting profiles of teens or young adults—is that MySpace is extremely customizable, so its users can really play with anonymity.

MySpace provides lots of ways to radically alter the appearance of a page, including changing the fonts and colors, and even removing or moving standard elements that are there by default (we cover this in Chapter 7). So if we tell you to click a box and you can't find it, it's not because you (or we) are getting senile. It's because the owner of that profile has done a "hack" to change things around (you'll find more on hacking in Chapter 7). Usually, if you look hard enough, you will find things like the person's Contacting box, but it may not look familiar at all.

Using MySpace Mail

Mail is your central MySpace communication tool. This email-like interface lives on your MySpace home page and lets you contact a user, receive notifications, and hear from friends and other MySpace users.

Unlike your regular email, MySpace mail is internal to the service. It's used by fellow MySpace users to communicate with one another and is not designed to send and receive messages across the Internet to users of other email services. By default, MySpace does send messages to your regular email account (your login email address), notifying you that you have mail, comments, blog posts, invitations, and so on waiting in your MySpace account. You can turn those notifications off in Account Settings if you want.

Whenever you log into MySpace, new mail messages are flagged in bold red in your My Mail box on the left side of your home page.

To read mail messages, follow these steps:

1. In the My Mail box on your home page, click the red New Messages! link or the Inbox link (**FIGURE 4.7**).

FIGURE 4.7 Click New Messages! to see what mail has come in.

2. Open the message by clicking the subject link.

3. Use the buttons at the bottom of the message screen to reply to the message or delete it.

Don't ask us why, but you don't send messages from your MySpace mail or even from your home page. To send a message, follow these steps:

1. On the profile page of the friend you want to contact, click Send Message in the Contacting box.

    A blank mail-message window, addressed to that user, opens (**FIGURE 4.8**).

    Remember, it's possible that the person may have *hacked*, or altered, the page, and you won't see or you might have trouble recognizing the Contacting box. Before you give up on contacting the person, look around carefully; the Contacting box with its eight links

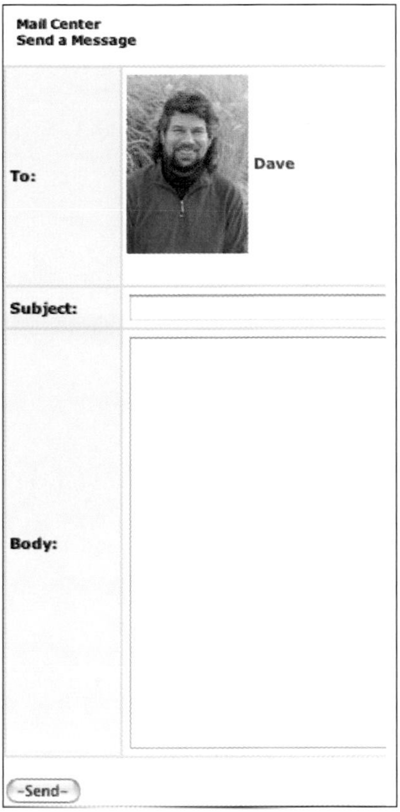

FIGURE 4.8 The message window, where you type your email.

(Send Message, Add to Friends, Instant Message, etc.) is probably still there. Even people who love spiffing up their profiles still want to receive messages from friends.

2. Type your message in the Body text box.

3. Click Send.

Sent messages are stored in the Sent box for 14 days, and you can check their status (whether the messages were sent, read, or replied to). Currently, this feature is a privacy issue, in that it makes spying easier: You can tell whether a user has read your message, and others can do the same when they view messages they've sent you recently. At this writing, Account Privacy Settings don't address this issue.

Kids are likely to get mail from people they don't know. As with all email, they should be careful about responding or clicking links in those messages that could take them to inappropriate Web sites, and they should be careful about responding to any offers that come via email.

Using the Address Book

MySpace offers an address book that lets you store information about your friends and other contacts.

To begin managing your address book, follow these steps:

1. Click the Manage Address Book link in the Hello box on your home page.

2. Use the Quick Add Contact feature to start building your address book (**FIGURE 4.9**).

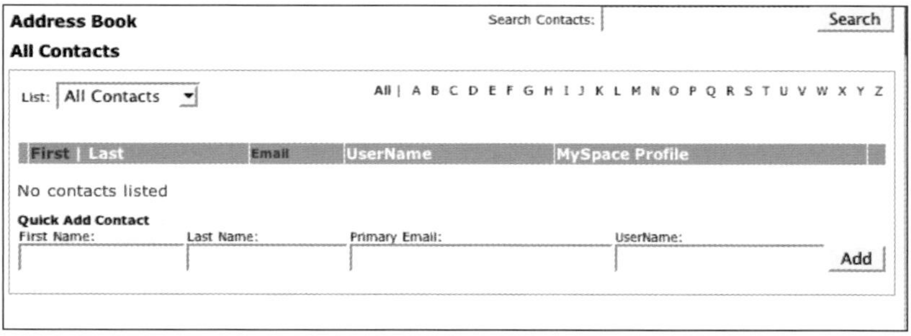

FIGURE 4.9 Fill in your friends' names and contact data to add them to your address book.

Populate the name, email, and user-name fields, and click Add. If you enter just the email address, the address book will populate the UserName field and MySpace page details field automatically.

3. You can add more information at any time by clicking the View a Contact link and then clicking Edit at the bottom of the screen (**FIGURE 4.10**).

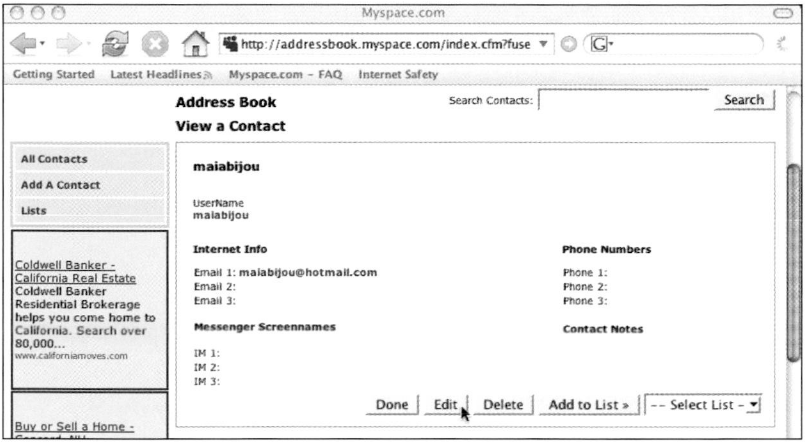

FIGURE 4.10 Edit your friends' contact info on the View a Contact page.

Using Bulletins

Bulletins are an easy way to contact or send news to several MySpace friends all at once.

To post a bulletin, follow these steps:

1. In My Mail (on your home page), click Post Bulletin. The Post Bulletin page appears.

2. Enter a Subject line, and write your message in the Body text box

3. Click the Post button at the bottom of the page. A confirmation screen appears.

4. Verify the posting, edit it, or cancel it (**FIGURE 4.11**).

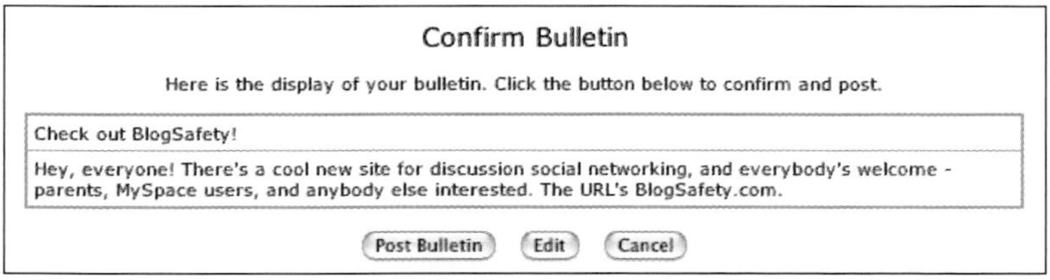

FIGURE 4.11 Confirm that you want to send this message to all your friends.

KEY PARENTING POINT

Mass bulletin posts are fairly common in MySpace culture. What MySpace users should remember—particularly those with numerous friends—is that these posts go out to everyone. For privacy and self-protection, remind kids not to reveal personal information, such as their email address, phone number, street address, or where they plan to hang out that night. It's also thoughtful to avoid spamming friends with too many messages.

Reading Bulletins

Because of the frequency of bulletin posts, MySpace doesn't notify users when a new one has been posted, unlike mail messages, comments, and new invites.

To check the latest bulletin posts, go to the My Bulletin Space on your MySpace home page. Bulletins are listed sequentially, starting with the most current posting.

To open and read a message, click the subject link in the Bulletin column (**FIGURE 4.12**).

Blocking Bulletins

Bulletins are great communication tools, but they can easily become annoying and spamlike. If you are receiving unwanted or excessive bulletins, the only way to block them is to delete the sender as a friend. To do this, open the bulletin, and click the Delete from Friends button on the bottom-right side of the screen.

Modifying Your Top 8

On MySpace, "Your Top 8" refers to the featured friends in your My Friend Space on your profile page. When you first join MySpace and start building your network, the first eight friends will automatically populate this window. As you make more friends, you can opt to prioritize who is in your Top 8.

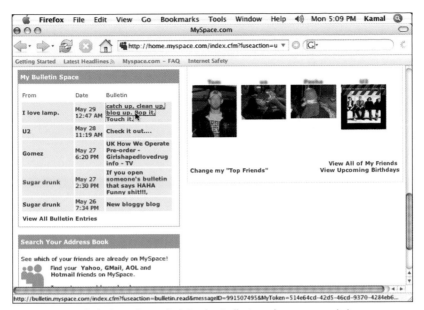

FIGURE 4.12 Click the subject link in the Bulletin column to read that message.

What this means varies from user to user. Some MySpace fans might feature all their top MySpace friends—those who actively socialize and participate online. Others might prioritize, based on their real-world friends, regardless of whether they are big MySpace users. Others try to balance all the key people in their life and evenly cover friends, family, and colleagues—or be really safe and top the list with their girlfriend, boyfriend, and siblings, and then be diplomatic and fill the rest of the slots with bands representing their favorite music. A workaround some MySpace users employ is to hack their profile to feature their "Top 20" or "Top 30" instead, or even to hide this section altogether. (For details about how to do this, see Chapter 7.)

In any case, the Top 8 list is very visible and can be a social minefield if not given much thought. Teens are usually very mindful of this, but the question of how they rank people on this list or how much they think about it could be an interesting parent-child talking point or even a teachable moment.

Deleting Friends

You can delete existing friends at any time by following these steps:

1. In the Friend area of your home page, click the Edit Friends link in the top-right corner (**FIGURE 4.13**).

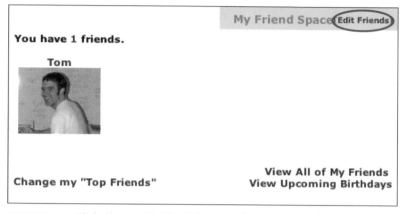

FIGURE 4.13 Click Change My Top Friends under the photo. (It does help to have more than one friend!)

2. On the Edit Friends page, check the box beside the photo of the friend you want to delete.

3. Click Delete Selected to delete that friend.

Friends whom you delete will *not* be notified about the deletion, though they will probably figure it out when you no longer appear as their friend.

Commenting on Other People's Profiles

Comments are in many ways the social glue of MySpace, and they provide a quick, fun, and popular way for online users to connect and stay in touch. As anyone who's visited a dorm knows, college students like to put things on each other's doors, and MySpace lets users do just that.

Unlike more private emails, these bulletin-board-like posts allow friends to publicly share thoughts, expressions, plans, and more—which means at times that people can learn a lot about your kids' personal business. Plus when someone posts a comment, it kind of reflects on the person whose page it's on.

We urge MySpace users who allow others to post comments to check their profiles often (if they don't already!) to make sure no one posted anything that invades their privacy, or is embarrassing or otherwise inappropriate. It's also a good idea to check friends' profiles to see whether and where comments about you show up.

Profile Comments

These comments are the most public of MySpace features, appearing as they do right on your main profile page.

You must be someone's friend to post a comment on his or her profile, and users can set Privacy Settings to require approval before posting (see Chapter 3 for more details). But if you have a public profile, almost anyone can view your profile and its comments, should he or she come across it.

To post a comment in a friend's profile:

1. On your friend's profile page, scroll to the bottom of the Friends Comments section, and click Add Comment (**FIGURE 4.14**).

2. Type your comment in the text box.

3. Click Submit.

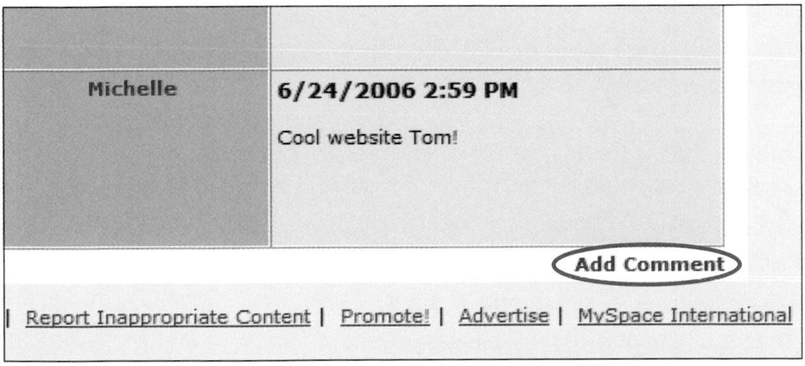

FIGURE 4.14 You can add a comment at the bottom of any friend's profile.

Picture Comments

MySpace picture galleries are another spot where you can share your thoughts and hellos. Users are allowed to upload a maximum of eight photos and images to their profile, and friends often like to comment on pics that catch their attention.

To add a picture comment:

1. On your friend's profile page, click the Pics link below the profile picture.

2. In the picture gallery, click the picture you want to comment on.

3. Click Post a Comment below the photo (**FIGURE 4.15**).

Larry as a baby

» **Post A Comment**
» **Report This Image**

0 Comment(s)

FIGURE 4.15 Click Post a Comment below the photo of choice.

4. Fill in the text box.

    A Confirm Comment screen will pop up.

5. Click Post Comment to publish the comment.

    If your friend has turned on commenting privacy, you will have to wait until your friend approves the comment before it displays.

Commenting and Privacy

To best protect your online self and reputation from potential unwanted comments and posts, you may want to consider enabling the Approve Comments Before Posting feature in the Privacy Settings section of your Account Settings.

This feature will allow you to review and approve all comments before anyone can see them. You'll be notified via email, and the user will receive a message, after they've posted a comment, saying you must approve their post first.

To activate this feature:

1. On your MySpace home page, click Account Settings and then click the red Change Settings link beside Privacy Settings.

2. Scroll down to My Privacy Settings, and check Approve Comments Before Posting (**FIGURE 4.16**).

3. Click Change Settings.

FIGURE 4.16 People can say anything they want in *your* profile unless you check Approve Comments Before Posting in your Privacy Settings.

Editing and Deleting Comments

Although only friends can write comments in users' profiles, blogs, and photos, there is always the possibility that someone will post something that's undesirable, embarrassing, inappropriate, or jeopardizes your teen's privacy. That's why users have the ability to delete comments that others put on their profiles.

If someone posts a comment you don't approve of, you can easily delete the posting.

To delete profile comments:

1. Under your picture in your Hello Box, click Profile.

2. Scroll to the Comments section of your profile and click View/Edit All (**FIGURE 4.17**).

3. Find the comment you wish to delete and click Delete Comment.

4. When MySpace asks you to confirm, click OK.

To delete unwanted comments people have posted about a photo or image you've posted in your profile:

1. On your home page, click Profile in the Hello box to display a page containing all your uploaded pictures.

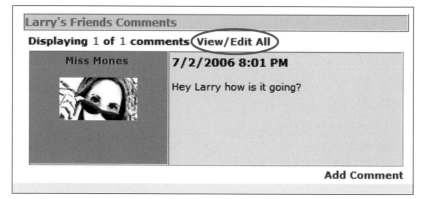

FIGURE 4.17 You can delete comments by clicking View/Edit All in the comments area of your profile.

2. To view and edit comments, click the applicable picture. The photo will appear with the comment next to it.

3. Click Delete to remove the comment.

TIP

If your Profile Settings are HTML-enabled, people can post pictures and images, as well as text comments. To delete these types of "comments," follow the steps in the previous list.

MySpace Events

MySpace Event invitations are other pieces of MySpace mail that may pop up in your or your teen's Inbox quite often. (Some bands and other groups send Invites to huge swaths of MySpace users.) These invitations might announce shows, concerts, or parties coming up—or friends may be forwarding to you the invites they get.

To view Event Invites at any time:

1. Click the Events tab on the blue navigational bar of any page.

2. Click the Event Invites link on the left side of the screen.

You can also find Event Invites in your regular MySpace inbox.

TIP

You can't turn off receiving these invites in your MySpace mail, but you can change your account settings so you don't get them in your regular (non-MySpace) email account. You can do this from Account Settings (in the Hello box on your home page) by checking the Do Not Send Me Notification Emails box, located beside Notifications.

To send an event invitation:

1. Click MySpace Events on the blue navigation bar of any page.

2. Click Create New Event.

3. Fill in the applicable fields, and click Invite & Update (**FIGURE 4.18**).

FIGURE 4.18 Fill in the message box and the email addresses of the people you want to invite.

4. On the next screen, you can opt to include a personal message, show the guest list to everyone, ask invitees to RSVP, import emails from the Hotmail or Yahoo! accounts of people you want to invite, or invite MySpace users.

5. Click Invit e and then click Update.

Photo Rankings

For better or worse, the Photo Rankings feature lets you rate the attractiveness or coolness of other people's photos. You or your teen can choose to submit them—or not. Ranking is on a scale of 1 to 10.

Adding your image to the rating system will allow other users to view and rate your image. Keep in mind that a person does not need to be your friend to comment.

To submit a photo for ranking:

1. On your MySpace home page, click Add/Edit Photos.
2. Select the photo you want to submit, and click the Add to Ranking button directly below it (**FIGURE 4.19**).

FIGURE 4.19 Select the photo you want ranked and click the Add to Ranking button.

To see what people think about your pic, go to your MySpace home page, and click the Ranking Score button.

Your Ranking Score is private and for your eyes only, though as mentioned earlier in this chapter, if you submit a picture, anyone can rank it.

To rank a MySpacer's picture, follow these steps:

1. Visit the user's profile, and click the Rank User link in the Contacting box.

    If the user has submitted a photo for ranking, you'll be taken to a window displaying the photo, as well as a ranking scale.

2. To vote, simply click the applicable number (**FIGURE 4.20**).

    If the MySpace user hasn't submitted a photo for ranking, you'll get a screen telling you this and suggesting that you contact them.

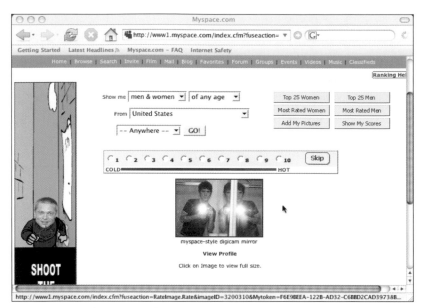

FIGURE 4.20 Submit your photo, and people can rate you on a page like this. Some people aspire to be in MySpace's Top 25 (among 80 million-plus!).

KEY PARENTING POINT

MySpace isn't the first site to include photo ratings. A lot of teenagers go to RateMe.com or HotorNot.com, among many other sites to submit their photos and be rated. While some teens might enjoy positive rankings, others could wind up feeling humiliated. Talk with your teen about whether or not you think it's a good idea to submit pictures for ranking and how you feel about their rating other people's pictures.

MySpace Communities

MySpace is all about "communities," be they a group of friends from the same city or school; people who have a common lifestyle, religion, or political viewpoint; or people who gather together around broader communities such as music, films, books, or a particular band, genre, author, or film. In other words, a community is anything that two or more people say it is.

Some communities are strictly virtual—most of the members probably have never met face to face—and others are an extension of real-life communities, such as those built around a particular school, church, sports team, or workplace.

We can't possibly write about even a fraction of the communities that have formed through the service, but we can talk about some of MySpace's major interest areas. The other thing we can't do is to point you to one screen or menu that lists all the communities, but we can help you find your way around.

Finding Community

One place to look for community is in the main navigation bar at the top of every page. There, you'll find links to Film, Videos, and Music. You'll also find links to Blog, which is where some people find community (in a more text-based way), and Groups, which is the natural spot for people gathering around specific topics.

Another place to look is the pale-blue box below the navigation bar on MySpace's home page (to get there, click the MySpace.com link at the top of any page). In that box, you'll find the many communities MySpace has added more recently: Comedy, Filmmakers, Games, Horoscopes, Movies, Music Videos, and Schools. That same box will take you to communities built around specific community tools: Blogs, MySpaceIM, Chat Rooms, and Groups (**FIGURE 4.21**).

All in all, community on MySpace is pretty much wherever you are.

Music

Music—and promoting independent musicians—has always been an integral part of MySpace. Music is the leading MySpace community and home to thousands of artists of every genre, from garage bands and indies to major recording artists, who have profiles complete with songs, bios, lyrics, and more (**FIGURE 4.22**). You'll find a link to the Music community on the blue navigation bar near the top of every page.

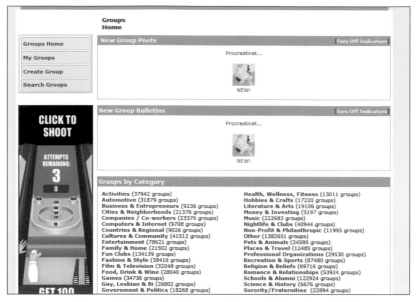

FIGURE 4.21 To get a feel for the sheer number and diversity of MySpace Groups, glance through the 222,683 groups under Music alone. (Music is the original MySpace interest group.)

FIGURE 4.22 MySpace Music's home page.

Founded as a platform for independent and startup artists to help them gain more exposure, this part of MySpace has become such a force and fan base that mainstream musicians are now participating as well, including Madonna, Shakira, and Keith Urban.

MySpace Music has become so huge that in November 2005, MySpace launched its own record label, called MySpace Records, and in January 2006, News Corp (the parent company) announced plans to launch a UK version of MySpace to cover the mega UK music scene.

Music profiles work pretty much the same as regular MySpace pages with a slight change in look and feel. Musicians can upload as many as three songs to their profiles; other MySpacers can choose to add these songs to their profiles as a personalization feature.

Film

Film is also a link on the main blue navigation bar. The Film community is a portal for independent filmmakers to gain exposure, to network and build fan bases, and to showcase their work. The functionality parallels that of MySpace Music and has features for indie filmmakers and fans, including a search function to locate filmmakers by role, location, film, or keyword; a list of top filmmakers by genre; and a list of screenings in your area.

You'll also find filmmaker forums, where the artists answer questions and discuss their films with fans. And just in case you or your teen wants to make it big on the big screen, there's a classified section with listings for industry jobs, auditions, casting calls, and more.

Books

There's a link to Books in the box just below the navigation bar on the MySpace.com home page. This section features book reviews, blogs, and featured book groups, as well as a Top Books section and search functionality. It's kind of like a regular book club, only virtual, and with lots more information, but no tea and cookies (**FIGURE 4.23**).

FIGURE 4.23 Your 24/7 virtual book club.

Comedy

You'll find a link to Comedy in the same box as Books. The section has a variety of humor-related content and interaction. Similar to the Music and Film portals, MySpace Comedy is a platform for comedians to gain exposure, network, and build a fan base, as well as another venue where users (and aspiring professional comics) can socialize.

Comedians can post profiles, list and search for gigs, and network in the forum. MySpacers can peruse forums and exchange jokes and funny stories; search for sketches, improv, and stand-up comedy shows; and check out the week's funniest MySpace video (**FIGURE 4.24**).

KEY PARENTING POINT

Hard as it is to imagine a comedian telling a dirty joke, there can be off-color comedy here that some parents may feel is inappropriate for teens. We recommend that you check out this forum firsthand and gauge whether you feel comfortable with your child's perusing the material.

FIGURE 4.24 For MySpacers seeking a little comic relief (or serious professional networking), check out the Comedy section.

Games

MySpace (or any cross-section of online life) would be incomplete without
a section devoted to video, online, and PC games. This type of interactive
entertainment is a big part of virtual communities and social networking, and
several classic multiplayer games (such as Dungeons & Dragons) have helped
spawn modern online social networks. MySpace Categories include sports,
action, trivia, TV shows (such as "Family Feud"), board games, and puzzles.

Games is basically a portal where gamers can connect, play solo, and
compete with other MySpace users.

Schools

The MySpace Schools community is a sort of after-school virtual hangout for high-school and college students and alumni, but its biggest and
most vocal group is clearly high-school students. College students are
more likely to hang out on Facebook (more on that in a moment). In case
you missed it, in Chapter 2 we talked about how high-school students

use MySpace and, as we hope we made clear, it is a vast network of communities of students most commonly socializing with friends at their own schools (**FIGURE 4.25**).

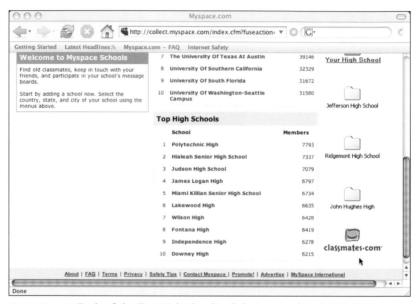

FIGURE 4.25 Each of the Top 10 high schools has more than 6,000 MySpace members!

Finding Classmates

A lot of kids use MySpace's search feature to find classmates from their school. Here's how:

1. On the main blue navigation bar near the top of any page, click Search.
2. In the Find Your Classmates section, type the school name, country, and state.
3. Click Find.

    A list of schools that meet your search requirements appears.
4. Click the name of the school to start your search.

You can narrow your search by gender; age range (starting with 16); marital status; dating status; whether they're current students or alumni; year of graduation; and even more options, such as major, clubs, and Greek affiliation.

Although this feature is primarily used by current students, Larry tried it out on his high-school graduating class of "a long time ago." Out of about a thousand people from his class, he found three classmates.

Locating School Groups

Schools have always been a powerful source of community, and so it is on the social-networking scene. If you have a school in your present or past, MySpace aims to have a forum for you, the service tells us.

Each school forum (also called a group) has its own moderator, who applies to MySpace for the job. "We personally review each school-moderator application form," a spokesperson from MySpace told us. The moderator's job is to keep the discussion appropriate and on topic (he or she can block users and delete posts). Classmates can also rate the moderator, and MySpace reviews those ratings; enough negative ones can get the moderator replaced. (MySpace staff stays in touch with school moderators.)

School forums have their own classified ads associated with them, so users can swap or sell textbooks, find bands for prom night, or hire a tutor. MySpace distinguishes between high-school classifieds (which don't include ads for roommates and apartments) and college-level ones (which do). Both current students and alums are welcome in the school forums.

If you want to locate your kids or any school group on MySpace, here's how:

1. Click Groups on the main navigation bar and then click Search Groups in the little blue box on the left.

2. In the Groups Advanced Search window, type the school's name.

3. Choose Schools *&* Alumni from the Category pull-down menu.

4. Choose the school's state from the State pull-down menu.

5. To narrow your search further, select a choice in the Miles From pull-down menu and fill in the zip code in the Zip box (**FIGURE 4.26**).

Groups that match your search are displayed. These could include a group of current students, an alumni group, the Class of 2002, or any other group associated with that school (**FIGURE 4.27**).

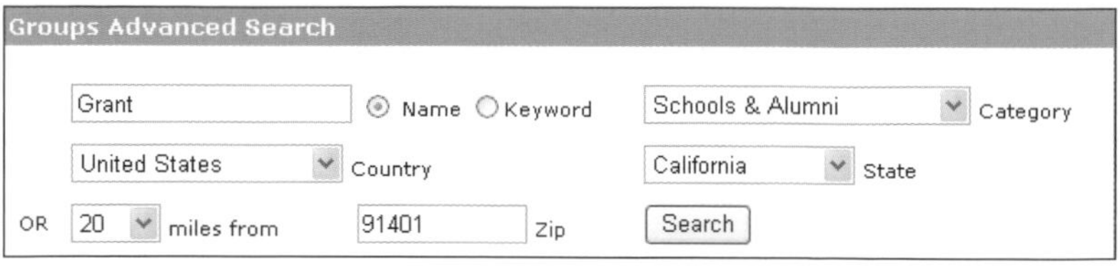

FIGURE 4.26 Type your school name and location information and make a choice from the Schools & Alumni category to find all the forums associated with your school.

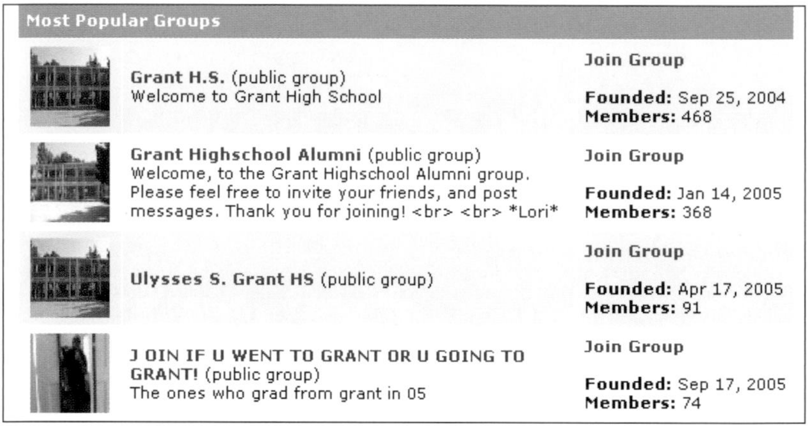

FIGURE 4.27 Here are some of the forums associated with Grant High School in Van Nuys, California (among other Grant High Schools around the country).

TIP

We found that you really need to type the school's zip code and choose a number from the Miles From pull-down menu (the Any option doesn't work) to zoom in on your school of choice. Specifying the state matters less than the zip code.

Facebook: The 'Other' Student Social-Networking Site

Although MySpace is certainly used by plenty of college students, another social-networking site, called Facebook, is very popular on college campuses (**FIGURE 4.28**). In fact, Facebook says it's on every four-year college and university campus in the United States.

FIGURE 4.28 The very spare Facebook home page.

Unlike MySpace, Facebook has an authentication system that makes it harder to be anonymous in this service. College students and staff members must use their .edu email accounts to sign up (and you get an .edu account only if you are associated with a college or university).

Facebook recently started offering its services to high-school students (who don't need .edu email addresses but must be invited by other students from their high school), as well as to employees of companies who have an approved company email address for Facebook.

Chat Rooms

A *chat room* is an online space where people "chat" by typing and sending short messages to people on the same page in real time. Entering a chat room is essentially the virtual equivalent of a cocktail party. You schmooze, socialize, *maybe* connect, and have extended conversations with one or more individuals, but in-depth conversations are rare, to say the least.

Because MySpace is a social network, chat rooms are a popular feature. There are numerous chat rooms in MySpace Chat, organized by categories and topics.

To log on to a chat room:

1. Go to the main MySpace home page by clicking the MySpace.com link (top-left corner of any page).

2. Click the Chat Rooms link in the pale-blue box just below the main navigational bar.

    You'll see three tabs, with options to search by categories, location, or age (**FIGURE 4.29**).

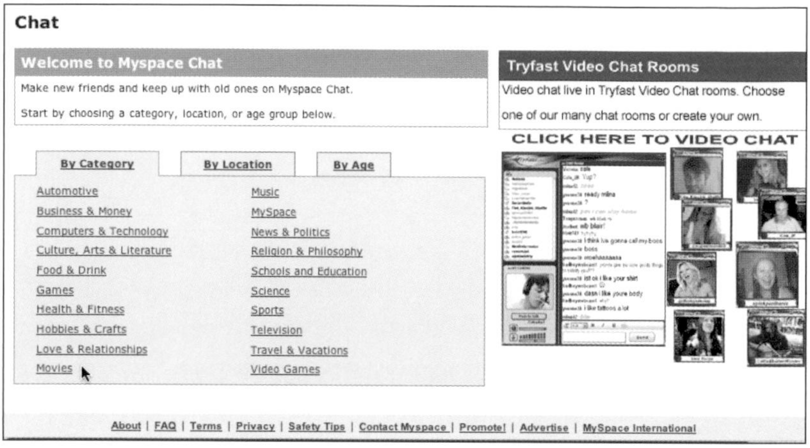

FIGURE 4.29 There are numerous chat rooms in MySpace Chat, organized by categories and topics, from Food & Drink to Automotive to Campus Life.

3. Click the desired tab and then a subtopic on that tab.

    You'll be logged into the applicable chat room automatically.

4. To start a conversation or announce your presence, type a short message in the text box on the bottom-right side of the page (next to Style) and then press the return key or click the Send button (**FIGURE 4.30**).

5. To leave a chat room at any time, just close the application window by clicking the X (located on the top right on Windows screens and top left on Macintosh screens).

KEY PARENTING POINT

MySpace does have moderators who, from time to time, check the chat rooms for disruptive and inappropriate behavior, but they're not working around the clock, and they're not in every chat room. Even if they're there, moderators can deal with problems only after the fact. So kids need to know what not to say and to be on the lookout for rude, obnoxious, and occasionally dangerous people.

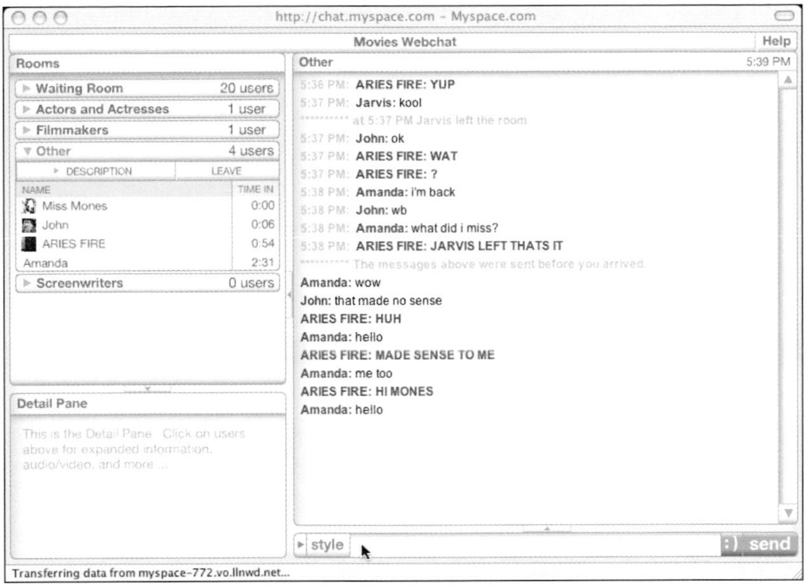

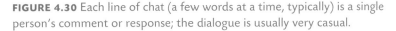

FIGURE 4.30 Each line of chat (a few words at a time, typically) is a single person's comment or response; the dialogue is usually very casual.

When you enter the room, you'll see streams of short messages among the visitors. You can read the threads and get the gist of what's going on or dive right in. Lots of people *lurk,* watching the conversation for a bit before jumping in. Typical online etiquette is to announce your presence with something like "Hi, people."

MySpace has age-related chat rooms for teens and people in their 20s, 30s, and so on. Having a space just for teens is a terrific idea—and the room is off limits to anyone whose stated age is older than 20—but there is nothing to stop older people from going into that room by lying about their age. There is also nothing to stop teens from entering rooms for older folks, even if they don't lie about their age.

Although there are moderators for some chat rooms, moderators don't patrol the rooms 100 percent of the time. We recommend that if at any time you notice disruptive or inappropriate behavior, you should just leave the chat room. To leave, simply close the application window. If you notice that some user is repeatedly causing a disturbance, and a moderator isn't intervening, you can file a complaint or report the user to MySpace Customer Care by clicking the Contact MySpace link at the bottom of every page (choose Report Abuse below Please Select a Topic in the Contact Request box).

KEY PARENTING POINT

Chat is not a great place for kids anywhere on the Internet, unless it's clearly designated for kids only and monitored 24/7 by responsible human beings (AOL's Kids Only is one example). This is because conversations in chat rooms can easily and quickly become sexually explicit. And tempers can flare in chat rooms; people can forget their manners (kind of like the way some folks act when they're angry while driving a car). When your kids are in a chat room, what they type can be seen immediately by everyone else in the room; there's no way to take it back. So warn them to be careful not to enter anything that personally identifies them or that they might later regret having said.

Let kids know that if they see something that's hurtful, they should try not to take it personally; it says more about the person saying it than about them. In general, MySpace profiles and blogs, where users have some editing control and are generally "talking" with their friends, are better for teens.

Forums

Forums are for holding discussions online and are great resources for questions, help, and advice. On other sites, they are commonly referred to as message boards, discussion boards, and bulletin boards.

Forums differ from chat rooms and instant messaging because they focus more on single topics, are generally more in-depth than chat, and don't encourage real-time personal interaction. Still, you need to be careful that you don't say anything inappropriate and have a thick skin in case someone else forgets to mind their manners.

To participate in MySpace Forums:

1. Click Forum on the blue navigational bar at the top of any MySpace screen.

    On the Forum home page, you'll see folders or categories with short descriptions (**FIGURE 4.31**).

2. Click the desired topic and scroll through the listed subtopics until you see one of interest.

| Home | Browse | Search | Invite | Film | Mail | Blog | Favorites | Forum | Groups |

Forum Home

Forum Category	Rooms	Topics	Posts
Automotive Talk about your ride. We did it for TheBoz.	Chat	25457	509751
Business & Entrepreneurs Need advice or a partner for your latest venture?	Chat	11288	43000
Campus Life Study partners, PARTIES, and alumni.	Chat	9450	58895
Career Center Career advice, discussion and opportunities.	Chat	7640	30910
Comedy Forums for comics and lovers of comedy.	Chat	1650	17686
Computers & Technology From PCs to iPods; technoid congregation.	Chat	20720	158628
Culture, Arts & Literature The finer things in life be here.	Chat	12566	116582

FIGURE 4.31 There are many topics and subtopics to choose among in these folders. (You'll note that there's chat on these subjects, too, but people usually don't stay on topic in chat.)

3. To post a topic, click Post a Topic (top-right corner), enter a subject, type your question or comment, and click Post This Topic.

    You'll see a Preview Topic confirmation screen.

4. Click Post This Topic to publish your comment.

5. Check back regularly to see how other MySpacers have responded to your post.

KEY PARENTING POINT

As we mention elsewhere in the book, we run a parents' forum about social-networking safety at BlogSafety.com. It's a great way to test out this technology and maybe pick up some tips from other parents in the process.

Instant Messaging

MySpace introduced an instant-messaging feature in June 2006 very similar to the popular AIM (AOL Instant Messaging) and Yahoo! and MSN (Microsoft) Messenger services (**FIGURE 4.32**). Unlike other aspects of MySpace that work within your Web browser, to use this service, you must download a separate piece of software. As of this writing, the MySpaceIM service works only with Windows (sorry, Mac users).

FIGURE 4.32 MySpaceIM works a lot like other instant-messaging services, so it'll be very easy for your kids to pick up (if they haven't already!).

To download the MySpaceIM program:

1. On the MySpace.com home page (not *your* home page), click MySpaceIM in the box just below the main toolbar.

2. Click the Download MySpaceIM link, which downloads an installation program that you can run to install the software.

Pay close attention to messages from your browser. You may have to select a security option to allow a download.

When the MySpaceIM software is installed, run the program, and fill in your email address and MySpace password just as you do when you sign into MySpace. The software can be configured to remember this information in the future.

Before you can start exchanging messages with friends, you have to add them to IM by clicking Add Your Friends to IM! just below your photo. You'll see a list of your friends, whom you can add by clicking their profile names.

Then, when you're signed on, you'll see a list of your friends who are online and also running the IM software. To send someone an instant message, double-click his or her name, and you get to a box where you can start typing your message.

KEY PARENTING POINT

Unless their parents use IM at work, most teens know more about instant messaging than we'll ever know, and even if we're fluent, they use it differently than we do—with multiple conversations and other tasks running simultaneously. It's tough to get a word in, but if you can, try to get teens to include only people they know personally in their IM friends lists—and to remember that people can copy and paste their comments elsewhere, beyond their control. They need to think before they post here, too.

There are some optional privacy features in MySpaceIM, which you can configure by choosing File > Preferences in the IM program and then clicking Privacy. Your choices allow you to be contacted by anyone or only people in your contact list (we recommend the latter, of course). You can also list specific people you want to block from contacting you.

While you're looking at Preferences, check out General Preferences, which give you control over what picture to display in IM, as well as control over some other features.

Also look at the Appearance options, which control how the IM program looks, and the Contact List options, which help you manage your contact list. You can also change the alerts and sound, which is a very good idea if you're using IM in an office or classroom, where you don't want others to hear sounds when you send and receive messages.

Blogging

This area of MySpace can be a bit confusing because, technically speaking, all of MySpace is a kind of feature-rich blogging tool. But the way the company handles blogs is to treat them as a separate feature. MySpace was one of the first social net works to make profiles the central focus. Blogs are optional, and from what we've seen, most kids don't bother with them, opting instead to use their profiles to keep up with their friends.

Blogs are more for people who are into written expression. Still, parents should be aware of blogging, because many kids do use it when they feel like being the host of an ongoing discussion (slightly more substantive, sometimes, than profile comments) or having their very own platform for sharing insights, writing, artwork, and more.

To set up a MySpace blog:

1. Click Manage Blog in the Hello box on your MySpace home page.

2. In the My Controls area on the left side of the page, select Post New Blog (**FIGURE 4.33**).

    The phrase *Post New Blog* can be misleading, especially to anyone who's worked with other blogs. You're not necessarily creating a new blog. What this option really means is that you're creating a new blog posting or entry.

3. Enter the requested information.

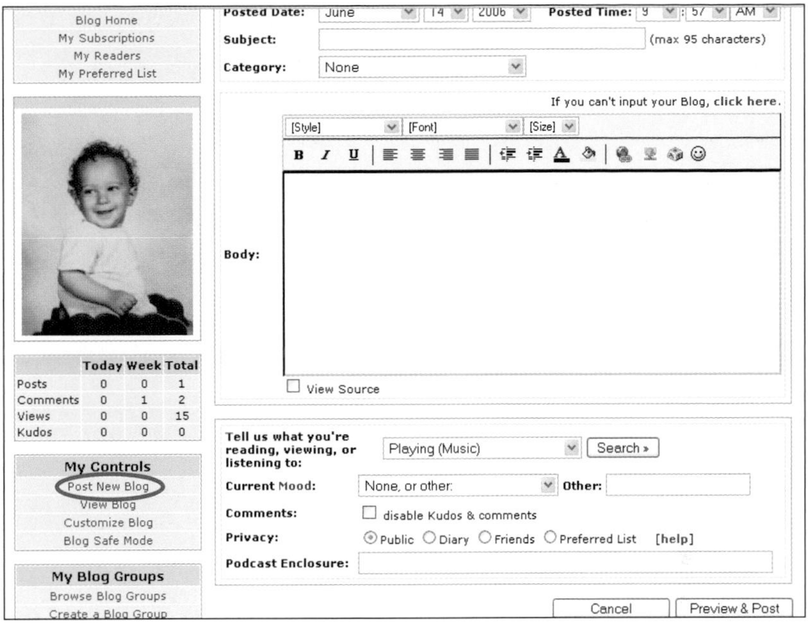

FIGURE 4.33 There are many options for giving your entry a little style.

4. Type your post in the Body section (or paste text from your word processor).

5. Add anything else you want, such as music and current mood.

6. Decide whether you want to allow people to comment and who you want to view the blog.

7. Click Preview & Post in the bottom-right corner.

You'll be able to preview what you've created before you actually post.

Blog Privacy

At the bottom of the Post a New Blog Entry screen is a place where you can designate whether each new entry is Public (readable by anyone), Diary (readable only by you), Friends (for your friends only), or Preferred List (which makes it available only to people you put on that list).

On the blog-entry page, you can also specify who is on your preferred list by clicking My Preferred List near the top-left side of the page, just above your photo. That same area has menu items that allow you to view who subscribes to your blog and to manage your subscriptions to other blogs.

You also can choose the Disable Kudos and Comments option so that others can't post items on your blog.

Blog Comments

If you have friends who regularly post to their blogs, you might occasionally read one and want to respond, start a discussion, or connect in some way.

To post a comment:

1. Scroll to the bottom of your friend's blog, and click Add Comment.

2. In the text box, write your message.

3. Click Post.

To delete unwanted blog comments:

1. Click View My Blog on your MySpace home page.

2. Select the offending blog posting.

3. Click the Remove link below it (**FIGURE 4.34**).

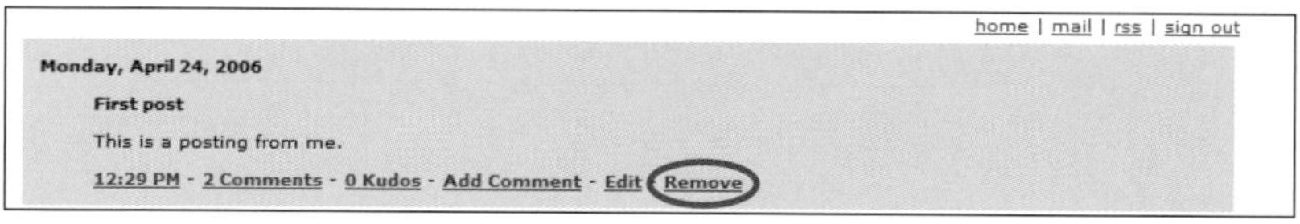

home | mail | rss | sign out

Monday, April 24, 2006

First post

This is a posting from me.

12:29 PM - 2 Comments - 0 Kudos - Add Comment - Edit Remove

FIG 4.34 Click the Remove link to delete a blog posting.

Blog Safe Mode

Listed under My Controls on your blog home page, Blog Safe mode allows you to view your HTML code in a blog without affecting formatting, so you can fix any problems. Because you need to know a bit of HTML to use it, this mode is really designed for advanced users. It's certainly not rocket science, but it is a more advanced feature that many users don't use. You can learn more about HTML in Chapter 7.

Tackling Safety Issues

By now, you're a MySpace "expert," at least compared with most parents. Knowing the basics of how to use the service is a great start. But now it's time to take your hands off the keyboard and start thinking about hands-on parenting in the digital age. In the next chapter, we talk about safety, but before you run and hide, at least read the first few pages. You might be pleased to learn that it's not quite as dangerous out there as some people might have you believe.

CHAPTER 5

Social Networking Safely

BASED ON RECENT NEWS REPORTS, you might think that something incredibly dangerous has burst on the scene—that there's a predator lurking behind nearly every keyboard waiting to sexually assault a teenager. Well, predators and tragic cases of sexual assault do exist, but before you yank the broadband modem out of the wall, consider the real risks.

We recently heard about a video that exposes the "current pandemic of sexual predation via the Internet" (from a company that offers a monitoring service), and plenty of other people are only too willing to tell you about the "growing epidemic" of kids who have been victims of Internet-related sexual exploitation. It's enough to scare a parent to death.

But despite a handful of truly tragic situations, the facts are that:

- The odds of your child being the victim of Internet-related sexual violence are extremely low.

- There are much more likely risks that the headlines often overlook.

Most news reports about MySpace in the first few months of 2006 concerned a handful of tragic cases involving men contacting teen girls on MySpace and persuading them to meet offline for sex. Then the number of school-related stories about threats to peers and teachers started growing.

We've also seen a few stories about identity theft on MySpace. Most of these stories concerned kids' user names and passwords—in other words, the peer-to-peer harassment we'll be hearing more about from the media as reporters move beyond the predation story.

First, the Research

Though statistics about risks in social-networking sites haven't been compiled, we do know some things about sexual predation online.

It's Usually Not 'Stranger Danger'

A 1994 study published by the University of New Hampshire (UNH) Crimes Against Children Research Center, the premier source of data on child exploitation, concluded that 70 percent to 90 percent of sexual abuse is committed by "persons known to the child." When the victim has been a girl, a third to a half of the crimes are committed by family members. When the victim has been a boy, 10 percent to 20 percent of the perpetrators are family members.

Detective Frank Dannahey, the youth officer in the Rocky Hill, Connecticut Police Department we mentioned in Chapter 2, told us that most of the sexual-assault cases he works on involve people the kids know. "I think probably the number of reports about MySpace we see in the media isn't an accurate representation of what really happens." Still, he feels kids need to understand the potential.

Dannahey appeared on "Dateline NBC" in April 2006 to illustrate how "stranger danger" can occur when teenage girls allow themselves to be deceived by a clever adult (in this case, himself) using a MySpace profile to pose as a teenage boy.

Deception Is Not the Norm

Many people believe that online sexual predators are usually older men posing as teenagers, but research suggests that's not the case. Another study published by UNH in 2004—this time about *Net*-related sexual-exploitation crimes against minors—found that only 5 percent of offenders tried to deceive victims about being older adults; only 21 percent misrepresented their sexual motives, and most of those deceptions involved promises of love and romance, not the offenders' ultimate objective.

Force Is Seldom Used

The 2004 study also found that only 5 percent of offenders used force, 16 percent used coercion, and 3 percent used abduction to sexually exploit their victims. This suggests that, in most cases where young people are victimized, the exploitation is consensual. The research also suggests that it may be misleading to categorize offenders in such cases as strangers, because victims and offenders had typically communicated, both online and by telephone, for more than one month prior to meeting in person.

Young Teens Are More Vulnerable

The 2004 study also found that 76 percent of the victims were between 13 and 15 years old, that 1 percent were 12 years old, and that no victim was younger than 12.

As for child exploitation in general, the number of reported cases of sexual assaults against children has actually gone down precisely during the time when Internet use among young people has exploded. On August 8, 2005,

USA Today reporter Wendy Koch cited government figures showing that "the rate of sexual assaults against adolescents ages 12 to 17 plunged 79% from 1993 through 2003, and the number of substantiated sex-abuse cases involving kids of all ages fell 39% in the same time period" (**FIGURE 5.1**).

FIGURE 5.1 A U.S. Department of Justice *Juvenile Justice Bulletin* explains reasons for the decline in child sexual abuse cases.

So far, virtually all the data about Internet sexual crimes against children come from studies done before the founding of MySpace and other social networking services (an update from UNH was expected right when this book went to press), but in terms of risk factors, researchers have told us that social networking is not much different from email, instant messaging (IM), and other online communication tools.

What we do know is that the number of actual sexual-exploitation cases is small relative to the millions of young people who use these sites. Let's take a hard look at the data.

Interpreting the Numbers

On April 6, 2006, an ABCNews.com subhead from a report on "Good Morning America" stated "Authorities Say 1 in 5 Children Has Been Approached By Online Predators" (**FIGURE 5.2**).

abc NEWS

GOOD MORNING AMERICA

All Sections | ↕   ABC News Home > Good Morning America

All Children Vulnerable to Online Predators

Authorities Say 1 in 5 Children Has Been Approached By Online Predators

RELATED STORIES

· Homeland Security Press Aide Held, Charged

· Teen Tells How He Was Lured Into Child Porn

abc NEWS

April 6, 2006 — Between the arrest of Brian Doyle, deputy pres secretary for the Department of Homeland Security, and the

FIGURE 5.2 A news report claiming that "1 in 5 kids has been approached by online predators."

If this statistic really is true, it would be reason enough for anyone to keep their kids from using the Internet. But we don't know of any authority who has explicitly said this. What the National Center for Missing & Exploited Children (NCMEC) has said is that "1 in 5 is sexually solicited online." But NCMEC never said that those solicitations were mostly from adult predators. The organization did disseminate the results of a scientific survey that includes that statistic ("1 in 5 is sexually solicited online"), but the study also showed the following:

- Many—probably most—of those solicitations came from other teens.

- "In 75 percent of incidents, youth had no or only minor reactions, saying they were not very upset or afraid in the wake of the solicitation."

- "None of the solicitations led to an actual sexual contact or assault."

The study in question was the frequently cited, landmark 2000 report "Online Victimization: A Report on the Nation's Youth," from the same highly regarded UNH research center we quoted earlier. That's the source of the oft-quoted "1 in 5" statistic.

Based on interviews with of 1,501 youth ages 10 to 17 who use the Internet regularly, authors David Finkelhor, Kimberly J. Mitchell, and Janis Wolak wrote that "approximately one in five regular Internet users (19%) said they had received an unwanted sexual solicitation or approach in the last year. Though not all of these episodes were disturbing to the recipients; however, 5% of users (one in four of those solicited) said they had a solicitation experience in which they were very or extremely upset or afraid, cases that we termed distressing incidents."

The report, which was commissioned by NCMEC, did highlight some very important safety issues for teens, but it didn't point to anything close to an epidemic of kids being preyed upon by adult predators.

In drilling down into the report, we noticed that fewer than a quarter (24 percent) of those solicitations came from people 18 and older (in 27 percent of the cases, their age was unknown), and that 1 in 33 (or 3 percent) of teens received solicitations that were "aggressive." The authors define aggressive as "a solicitor who asked to meet them somewhere; called them on the telephone; or sent them regular mail, money, or gifts."

Thirty-four percent of those aggressive solicitations were from adults. When you do the math (34 percent of 3 percent), you'll find that when it comes to adult-to-teen aggressive solicitations, the number is actually about 1 in 100.

That's still too high a number. When it comes to crimes against children, the only acceptable number is zero. But while we must always be vigilant about adults that prey on children, we shouldn't let that risk keep us from addressing more likely risks, including teen-to-teen sexual solicitations, which, in a small number of cases, can also be extremely disturbing or even dangerous.

Before you latch on to these statistics, however, remember they're from a study that, as of this writing, is more than six years old. UNH's update is expected to be released shortly after this book is published. If you want to read it, check our Web sites—BlogSafety.com and NetFamilyNews.org—for updates, along with other family-tech news.

When we spoke with Wolak, one of the authors of the 2000 and 2004 studies, she said, "What puts kids at risk is when they talk about sex with people they meet online. But the vast majority of kids won't get involved in that type of situation."

All of which tells us that most teens, at least to some extent, say they're practicing what we safety experts are preaching: not responding to these sexual messages. Or, as a teen would say, they're "ignoring the posers."

KEY PARENTING POINT

We think it's worth repeating Wolak's point for emphasis: "What puts kids at risk is when they talk about sex with people they meet online." Kids should be cautious about all messages from strangers and ignore or block any such messages that are sexual in nature. The sender can't hurt your child if there is no response.

Actions Speak Louder. . .

Having said that, we need to look not just at what teens say about online safety but what they do. Dr. Daniel Broughton, a pediatrician and professor at the Mayo Clinic College of Medicine who served for 13 years as Chairman of NCMEC, told us about an Internet-safety talk he gave at a high school in Rochester, Minn. After his talk, he participated on a panel with five students—four of them use MySpace—and he had this to say: "All of the kids said that they would not be so stupid as to communicate with people online that they didn't know, but later, when asked about what they like about MySpace, they all said that it lets them meet people from all over the country."

The April 26, 2006 NBC "Dateline" program that featured Detective Frank Dannahey made the same point. Detective Dannahey set up a MySpace profile claiming to be a 19-year-old named Matt who had just moved into town. With very little effort, he persuaded more than 100 people to add him to their MySpace friends list. Three of those "friends"—teenage girls from Middletown, Connecticut—appeared on the program. Prior to meeting "Matt," all three of the girls said that they do take precautions. One girl said, "You don't put, like, your full name out there. You know, where you live. I don't add people I don't know. I don't, you know, talk to people I don't know," and the others agreed. Another girl told Dateline, "if people, like, talk to me that I don't know, then I just— I just don't talk to them."

When "Matt" walked into the room, the girls were shocked to discover that he was actually an adult police officer. Based on what he learned about them online, Detective Dannahey was able to show the girls (and the TV audience) that he knew their full names, birthdays, where they lived, and where they hung out after school. And these are girls who thought they were being careful.

Assessing the Risks

The most extreme risks, in terms of consequences, generally are the least likely, but that's no reason to abandon caution. Although the chances of your child's being forced into a physically abusive situation as a result of an online encounter are low, online socializers face other dangers: the kind of stuff that has been going on in school lunchrooms, locker rooms, bathrooms, and parking lots for generations. Now it happens online, too—everything from pranks and mean gossip to insults, threats and impersonation, to compromising party videos and overexposure, to self-published child porn.

Kids are also being exposed to a constant barrage of sexually charged images from the profiles and Web sites of other teens on social networks, as well as in the ads and programming of conventional media.

"The more often a person is exposed to these themes, the more normal it seems and the more desensitizing it becomes," said Dr. Sharon Cooper, forensic pediatrician and adjunct Professor of Pediatrics at the University of North Carolina. Dr. Cooper also worries about some of the language that is becoming commonplace in popular culture. "Kids have started referring to themselves in sexually derogatory terms associated with prostitution."

Most of these dangers aren't life-threatening, but in some cases they can have an enormous impact on a child's self-esteem and, potentially, his or her future. Cyberbullying is the most common "risk" for middle-school-age social networkers. And privacy and protecting reputations is the biggest issue for high-school-age kids and college students.

Let's look at some of the more dangerous risks, beginning with the ones we fear most.

Adult Predators

Physical molestation, along with abduction, is a parent's worst nightmare. What we know about this terrible scenario is that abduction and rape resulting from an online encounter are highly unlikely.

The most likely online scenario leading to a sexual encounter, according to UNH's Crimes Against Children Research Center and interviews with analysts at the National Center for Missing & Exploited Children, is that children will be *lured* into an online encounter with a person they meet online and then persuaded, perhaps over time, to meet that person offline and engage in sexual activity. Although such activity may legally and morally be classified as statutory rape, in situations involving a minor and an adult, the sexual activity is rarely forced.

KEY PARENTING POINT

Kids may be naïve about the consequences of having sex with an adult but not necessarily blind to what they are doing. Only a small minority of offenders hide their intentions, as we mentioned earlier in the chapter. So for parents and law enforcement officials, a big part of the battle is not so much protecting kids against attack as protecting them against their own misjudgment.

To prevent our children from becoming compliant victims, we need to teach them to be alert when in public online and to understand the risks of engaging in communications with people they don't know. That requires critical thinking and an understanding about how people try to manipulate children in seemingly benign ways.

Though this may seem more challenging than just teaching children to avoid physically dangerous situations, instilling mere awareness (of potential manipulation and danger) in them can go a long way toward ensuring safe, constructive social networking online and also in their off-line encounters.

How Predators Groom Their Victims

Predators can be extremely skilled and patient, taking the time to groom their victims by paying them compliments or offering an understanding shoulder to lean on. In some cases, they also try intimidation.

Some of the things that predators say may look similar to what real friends might say, but if your kids get comments or questions like these from someone they don't know, they should recognize them as signs to be a bit suspicious.

We've developed some "lines" that can help parents and kids recognize predators. These lines are based on our own observations and on a report on cyberstalking and grooming published in June 2004 by the University of Central Lancashire in the United Kingdom. "Cyber Stalking, Abusive Cyber Sex, and Online Grooming" identifies common grooming techniques, and is based mostly on the kind of grooming that goes on in chat rooms:

- **"Where's your computer in the house?"** If the answer is "my bedroom," it tells the person that the parents are less likely to be in the room.

- **"What's your favorite band/designer/film/gear?"** Questions like these tell the groomer more about a child so that the groomer knows what gifts to offer: concert tickets, a Webcam, software, clothes, CDs, and so on.

- **"I know someone who can get you a modeling job."** Flattery, groomers figure, will get them everywhere.

- **"I know a way you can earn money fast."** This line is one of the tactics that snagged 13-year-old Justin Berry, into what became his Webcam prostitution business, which Kurt Eichenwald wrote about in the *New York Times* on December 19, 2005 ("Through His Webcam, a Boy Joins a Sordid Online World").

- **"You seem sad. Tell me what's bothering you."** This line is a sympathy schtick that can help turn a predator into a confidant.

- **"What's your phone number?"** Asking for personal info of any kind usually happens at a later stage, after the target is feeling comfortable with the groomer. All kids who go online should know not to give out personal info online.

- **"If you don't [do what I ask], I'll [tell your parents *or* share your photos in a photo blog, Webcam directory, or file-sharing network]."** Intimidation usually begins later, as the groomer learns more and more about the target.

- **"You are the love of my life."** This line is what "Amy," 15, fell for before traveling out of state to meet someone who'd groomed her (quoted in "Amy's Story," a 2002 feature article in the Teens section of NCMEC's Netsmartz.org).

Surveys and Questionnaires

One way to teach awareness is to explain to kids how predators groom their victims. One predator technique is to harvest as much information as possible about kids so that they can more easily manipulate them. Too much information makes the predator's job way too easy.

For example, surveys can provide an enormous amount of material at one glance. MySpace encourages users to complete an official profile questionnaire that asks about interests and favorite music, movies, and TV shows, as well as religion, habits, and sexual preference. Kids do not have to fill out these questionnaires. Some kids actually (probably wisely) fictionalize their answers to throw off observers who aren't their friends.

There are also some very popular third-party surveys that kids can fill out and post to their pages. Some of these surveys ask a lot of personal questions about likes, dislikes, personal feelings, drug and alcohol use, and sexual practices. The answers to such questions, if viewed by a would-be predator, could be used to exploit potential victims. In general, these surveys are not endorsed by MySpace but can be inserted into a profile using HTML code (see Chapter 7 for examples of these surveys and more information).

Special Risks for Some Kids

One size never fits all. And while our general advice applies to the vast majority of kids, it doesn't apply to everyone. That's where parents come in. It's your job to assess your child's unique needs and proceed accordingly.

There are some teens that are particularly vulnerable and may need a bit of extra attention from parents when they're online. Adrien Survol Rivin, a clinical social worker from Los Angeles who specializes in treating adolescents, worries about kids who are very compliant. "Children who are compliant in the real word," according to Rivin, "are more likely to act out by being non-compliant when they're online."

Part of being non-compliant is taking chances, such as entering into conversations with people they meet online. But, when under the influence of a predator, such children revert back to their old compliant selves because, says Rivin, "that's what they're used to, and they don't know how to be anything but compliant."

Paradoxically, she also worries about the "perfect kid." "If a kid is being perfect it may be that there are things that can't be expressed, so they have to go outside of the real word to find a place to break out of that mold. Often there is a certain level of excitement and danger that goes along with this." Predators know how to take advantage of such children, giving them the acceptance that they seek. Another issue with "perfect kids," said Rivin, is that "parents tend not to worry about them. They're excelling in school, music, sports and other activities, so it's easy for a parent to assume that everything is fine."

Still, says Dr. Richard Toft, a Palo Alto, Calif., child psychologist, "most kids are capable of knowing where to draw the line between online and offline relationships. There is a point were you have to move your body out of that chair and into the street, and that's a big step that most kids just won't take."

Harassment and Cyberbullying

Harassing peers in the process of figuring out where one stands in the social pecking order is nothing new. It's mostly a pre-teen and young-teen phenomenon. Cyberbullying is its online version, and it has become just as serious. It can include teasing kids about their appearance, sexuality, or other attributes; attempting to embarrass a child through the use of text, photos, video, and other media; and in some cases, threats and physical intimidation. There have been cases of kids creating Web sites with the sole purpose of harassing other kids and even trying to taunt them into committing suicide. Bullying can take place via email, chat rooms, IM, Web sites, interactive online games, social-networking sites, and cell phones. Sometimes, it spills over into the "real world."

Dealing with cyberbullying can be tough. In some cases, school officials or police can help, but if no laws are being broken, the police can't step in. Sometimes, too, the offensive behavior falls under the rubric of free speech.

One thing is for sure: Your kids need to understand that if they're mistreated by others, it's not their fault.

Advice for Dealing with Cyberbullies

The Canadian Web site Cyberbullying.org recommends the following tips for kids in dealing with bullying online:

- **Don't reply to messages from cyberbullies.** Even though you may want to respond, this is exactly what cyberbullies want. They want to know that they've got you worried and upset. They are trying to mess with your mind and control you—to put fear into you. Don't give them that pleasure.

- **Do not keep this to yourself!** You are *not* alone, and you did *not* do anything to deserve the bullying. Tell an adult you know and trust about the situation.

- **Inform your Internet service provider (ISP) or cell phone service.**

- **Inform your local police.** Do this with a parent's help, if the behavior seems to call for it. *(continued on next page)*

- **Do not erase or delete messages from cyberbullies.** You don't have to read the messages, but keep them; they are your evidence. Unfortunately, you may get similar messages again, perhaps from other accounts. If they're involved, the police, your ISP, and/or your cell phone service can use these messages to help you.

Don't Let Your Own Kids Be Cyberbullies

Most cases of cyberbullying involve kids as perpetrators as well as victims, so it's important to make sure that your kids aren't bullying others.

In "A Parents' Guide to Cyberbullying and Cyberthreats" (Center for Safe & Responsible Internet Use, December 2005), author Nancy Willard recommends that parents discuss with their kids "the value of treating others with kindness and respect and about your expectation that your child will act in accord with these values online." She also recommends that parents institute repercussions and enforce them when their child "engages in irresponsible online behavior."

Privacy and Security

We discussed in Chapter 2 the issue of teens laboring under what may be a false sense of privacy and security. To them it may seem like this is just "teen space" but it's not. Even kids who say they never give out personal information in chat rooms have told us they feel more comfortable revealing that information on MySpace, even though what they post can be seen, used, or shared by virtually anyone (unless they have a private profile).

Though we suspect that this situation is changing because of the enormous publicity about social-networking risks, we have spoken with numerous teens who still feel that MySpace truly is their space. Kids who told us that they would never post personal information in a chat room have argued that that rule shouldn't apply to social-networking sites, as though these sites somehow had a greater level of security than chat rooms.

But that's simply not true. Unless your kids have a private profile (which is now an option for all users and the default for 14 and 15 year olds), much of what they post on MySpace can be seen by virtually anyone. So even if their intentions are to communicate with their friends, they need to be aware that they have more "friends" than they realized.

What teens post in online public spaces without regard for their privacy and future prospects is the social Web's most common risk for high-school-age and college-age people. Parents are right to be concerned about this because, as of this writing, there isn't much evidence that teen social networkers are thinking about it enough: Young people need to think before they post. They need to consider whether they want a prospective employer, for example, to see what they're posting about themselves and their friends. Google, Yahoo, and MSN search aren't the only places where people can search for them. Social-network search boxes aren't just used to find friends, but also potential college recruits, employees, or anyone doing "background checks." There's also a permanent Internet Archive (more about that in a minute).

What kids need to think about (and parents can help them think about) is the "you-can't-take-it-back" issue. Once something's on a Web site or sent to a friend via cellphone, IM, or email, it's out of their control.

A friend can copy 'n' paste, pass it along, or upload it to a myriad of sites and services. It may be something a friend shares unthinkingly, or it might be passed along as a joke or maliciously, by an ex-friend who somehow got the originator's IM or email password.

KEY PARENTING POINT

For younger MySpacers, it would be ideal for parents to be on their kids' friends lists, the better to monitor what's going on in their online social lives. But at least consider a family rule that friends lists are only for people whom both the children and a parent know in real life.

Privacy is Double-Edge Sword

In June 2006 MySpace changed its privacy policy to allow anyone, including users 16 or older, to create a private profile.

Though we agree that people should have the right to privacy features, it's also important to point out that privacy is a double-edge sword. The upside is that privacy features can make your child's profile visible only to people on his or her friends list.

The downside is that parents may want to see their kids' profiles too. They need to be aware that privacy features can also block them unless they're on their kids' friends lists. There have been some calls to require social-networking sites to notify parents when minors set up a social-networking profile, but as of this writing we are not aware of any specific legislation, nor are we sure how it would work.

A public profile makes it harder for kids to carry on underground conversations, which can support or reinforce destructive behaviors such as anorexia, self-mutilation, discrimination, violence, or alcohol or drug abuse in kids who are troubled and seeking that kind of "support."

You may have heard about one well-publicized case in Kansas, in which five teenage boys used their public MySpace accounts to trumpet their intention to shoot up their school. An adult woman in North Carolina spotted the page and alerted authorities, who found the boys' weapons. A few media reports actually "blamed" MySpace, but the public MySpace profile and the alert woman might actually have helped prevent a tragedy. Of course, MySpace and other social networks aren't the only places where troubled teens can get reinforcement from kids with similar inclinations.

The Permanent Internet Archive

Even when no one goes out of the way to hold on to what you post, it can still hang around forever. Google, for example, has a temporary "cache" of Web pages that have been changed or deleted. There's also a site called the "Internet Archive" (archive.org) that is archiving almost everything on the Web to "offer permanent access for researchers, historians, and scholars," the site says. It doesn't matter to them that your kid's MySpace profile isn't the Gettysburg Address. It's part of the Internet and, thanks to this nonprofit service, it's potentially enshrined forever (**FIGURE 5.3**).

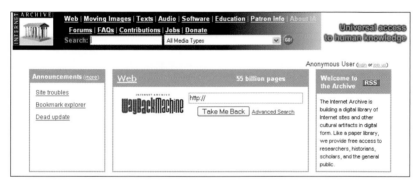

FIGURE 5.3 The Internet Archive's "WayBackMachine" can resurrect 55 billion defunct Web pages.

People can ask the archive to remove their pages, providing they have those pages' URLs. If kids find their pages (by typing the URL into the archive's search box on its home page), they can email the archive (see its FAQ) with the URL, requesting deletion. Allow for "about a two-day turnaround," the Internet Archive's spokesperson told us.

Phishing and Malicious Software

Many kids have access to credit or debit cards that should be shared only with legitimate merchants. Children as well as adults can fall victim to *"phishing"* schemes, in which they get an email that appears to come from a legitimate organization but that contains links to a rogue Web site (one that is not what it appears to be or says it is). Information that you provide to a rogue site can be used to steal your identity, break into your online accounts, and/or withdraw money from your various accounts. Kids should also be reminded never to give out their social

security numbers to anyone without checking with their parents
(**FIGURE 5.4**).

FIGURE 5.4 This looks just like PayPal's home page, but the URL at the top
doesn't say paypal.com. Any information you type could well go to a criminal
who can use it to break into your account.

There is even the risk of phishing within social networking. One visi-
tor to our BlogSafety.com forum reported that his son visited a profile
containing a link to a picture or video. When the boy clicked the link, what
looked like a MySpace page popped up, saying, "You need to be logged in
to do that." So he logged back in (or thought he did). But instead of giving
his password to MySpace, he unknowingly gave it to a fake site that looked
just like MySpace, meaning that his personal info fell into the hands of
criminals. Someone used the young man's account name and password

to impersonate him and create a malicious profile about him on another Web site.

KEY PARENTING POINT

Whether a phishing attack comes via email, IM, MySpace, or any other means, the safest way to log into a Web site where you're asked for a password, credit card numbers, or any other confidential information is to type the Web address (URL) of the site yourself, rather than clicking on a link to it.

The Art of Creating a Password

Many people worry about hackers stealing passwords, but in reality, many people in effect give them away by being careless.

Common mistakes are choosing passwords that are easy to guess, using the same passwords for all the sites you visit, and sometimes allowing other people to know your passwords. We know of a case in which a 13-year-old girl emailed sexually explicit photos of herself to a boy who had shared his email password with a "friend." That friend proceeded to find the photos and post them on a public Web page he created just to hurt the girl's reputation.

One simple way to pick a hard-to-guess password is to make up a phrase you can remember but others would never guess, and then base your password on letters and numbers from that phrase—for example, a phrase like "I started Kennedy High School in '03" to generate the tough-to-guess password IsKHSi03. It's also a good idea not to use the same password on all sites and definitely not to use important passwords (such as the MySpace one) on sites you don't fully trust.

KEY PARENTING POINT

Tell your kids why it's important not to let their friends have their passwords. Friends don't always stay friends—and they can be careless with passwords and share them with people your kids may not even know. Friends can also play pranks (like sharing very personal info from or impersonating someone who shared their password) and get people in trouble, mistakenly or to be mean—such as the case of the 13-year-old girl we just mentioned.

Updates and Security Software

We won't go into a lot of detail here, but everyone who uses the Internet should protect their PC by making sure it has the latest updates and by using security software that helps prevent a variety of problems, including viruses, spyware, and worms that install code that takes control of your PC or steals your passwords and credit card info. Windows security programs are available from a variety of companies, including McAfee, Microsoft, Trend Micro, and Zone Alarm. Symantec offers security software for both Windows and Macintosh (**FIGURE 5.5**).

You'll find more security tips at www.blogsafety.net/parentbook.

FIGURE 5.5 Microsoft's Windows Update page at update.microsoft.com automatically scans Windows PCs to make sure they have the latest security updates.

Legal Risks and School Policies

Kids aren't just victims of crime and harassment; they can be perpetrators as well. Kids need to be reminded that there are consequences to their online behavior. In addition to being wrong and rude, using the Internet to harass or annoy others can get your kids into trouble with school authorities or even the law. Kids should also know that there is a line between online "flirting" and sexual harassment that should not be crossed. Most parents have a pretty good idea where that line is, so as uncomfortable as it may be, it's a good idea to talk with your kids about it.

The same is true of other online infringements, such as hacking, invading others' privacy, planting viruses, or posting libelous or slanderous information, as well as copyright infringements. Young people also need to be aware that what they post on the Net can be used against them, now or in the future. There are numerous cases of police and school officials taking actions against young people based on information posted on MySpace and other social networks or revealed in chat rooms or via email.

For example, the Associated Press reported in April 2006 that two teenage boys in northern California were arrested for possession of "destructive devices" after posting a video on MySpace showing them firebombing an empty airline hanger ("Teens arrested after posting alleged firebombing video on MySpace.com"). And some colleges and high schools monitor MySpace and Facebook profiles for evidence of underage drinking or illegal drug use.

Parents and kids should check the Internet-use policies that apply in their schools. Schools have already taken action against students for posting things that administrators considered to be inappropriate. In the October 26, 2005, issue of the *Boston Globe*, writer Sarah Schweitzer reported a case in which the head of the student government association at Fisher College in Boston was expelled for comments about a campus police officer that he posted to his Facebook account. A school spokesperson told the *Globe* that the young man "was found to be in violation of the Student Guide and Code of Conduct."

Some schools ban school-based social networking outright. Although we don't necessarily agree with such a policy, students at those schools should know about it and its consequences.

Exposure to Inappropriate Material

Posting or viewing text, photos, and videos that are inappropriate for children is less an issue on MySpace and most legitimate social-networking sites than it is on the Web in general.

First, MySpace policy prohibits "photographs containing nudity, or obscene, lewd, excessively violent, harassing, sexually explicit or otherwise objectionable subject matter." Of course it's possible for such material to sneak past the company's censors, but if it's found, it's removed.

Second, we're not saying there isn't material in MySpace that some parents would find objectionable for their teens, but there are plenty of other places on the Net where teens are more likely to find this material.

A lot has been said and written about exposure to material (such as pornography) that can be considered "harmful to minors." Congress has gotten into the act several times with laws designed to protect kids against pornography and Web sites that are violent or hateful, or that advocate dangerous or illegal activity. In most cases, these laws have been challenged in court, and in many cases, they've been struck down for being overly broad and unconstitutional based on the First Amendment's protection of free speech.

Online pornography is a multibillion-dollar business, and although many porn sites require credit card access for much of their material, there is plenty out there that kids can find for free, including photos, stories, and videos. There are even pornographic videos that can be downloaded to iPods and game players.

Child Pornography

Although any form of pornography can be disturbing, especially if seen by young children, there is a legal (and, we would argue, moral) distinction between adult pornography and child pornography. Most sexually explicit material on the Internet is legal, but an exception is pornography that meets the following conditions, according to the National Center for Missing & Exploited Children's CyberTipline:

- "Depicts a minor engaging in sexually explicit conduct and is obscene"

or

- "Depicts an image that is, or appears to be, of a minor engaging in graphic sexual activity . . . whether between persons of the same or opposite sex, and such depiction lacks serious literary, artistic, political, or scientific value."

Federal law makes this type of material illegal in every state, and it's also illegal in many other countries. If you or your children come across such material, you should report it at once to the CyberTipline by visiting www.cybertipline.com or calling 800-843-5678.

KEY PARENTING POINT

We've noticed a small but growing number of "self-published child porn" cases. That's our term for when kids take sexually explicit and/or nude photos of themselves and email, IM, or upload them to Web sites, often with no concept of the potential impact on their lives if this material is passed around. Federal laws haven't caught up with this new phenomenon, and prosecutors around the country are wrestling with the issue. But according to Mary Leary, deputy director of the National Center for Missing & Exploited Children's Office of Legal Counsel, "Kids face the possibility of charges much more so now than in the past."

If Your Kids Are Viewing Porn . . .

Adult pornography, although legal, can be disturbing. But how you respond to a child's exposure to it should depend on several factors, including the age and maturity of your child, how he or she encounters it, how much time is spent looking at it and how it is affecting your child.

Overreacting generally is the worst response, because it tends to make kids take cover and become less communicative at a time when communication is really needed.

What's a Parent to Do?

In addressing a worried nation on the eve of his first term in office, President Franklin D. Roosevelt famously said, "The only thing we have to fear is fear itself—nameless, unreasoning, unjustified terror which paralyzes needed efforts to convert retreat into advance."

His advice couldn't be more relevant. Fear does paralyze. Parental fears shut down communication and make teens want to be as far away from their parents as they can possibly get. It has never been more important for that *not* to happen.

Trust between parent and child is needed more now simply because of the enormous number of options kids have online, with no mitigating factor or fallback *but* their parents. The bottom line: Because there are so many "places" they can go online that we don't know about, the best way to know about where they're going—the one that fosters trust and cooperation—is if they tell us about them.

This chapter has hopefully provided you a hype-free consideration of the research on online child exploitation; a clear-eyed view of all the risks associated with young people's use of the Web past and present; and what's newly risky on Web 2.0.

In the next chapter, we'll give you the "toolkit"—some tips, tools, and our best sense of how to parent young explorers of the social Web.

CHAPTER 6

A Parents' Toolkit

AT THE RISK OF seeming overly simplistic, the best way to protect your kids on MySpace or anywhere else is to talk with them—not only about risks, but also about the positive things they do online, what they do and don't like about social networking, and how you feel about it. Keep in mind they don't need us (or our credit cards) to use MySpace, but, as is usually the case in teenage lives, they need us as a sounding board.

It's important that your communication with your child is two-way—listen to them, be supportive, and keep an open mind. Whatever you do, don't overreact, and try to keep a sense of proportionality. In most cases, the first response to a problem shouldn't be to punish kids or even ban their use of MySpace or the Internet, but to discuss the issue to see whether there are solutions you can agree on.

Keeping kids safe online isn't about technology; it's about parenting. You know how to do that, regardless of how tech savvy you are (or aren't).

Kids Want Parental Input

Some people think kids don't value their parents' opinions, but data suggests that this isn't true. Boys & Girls Clubs of America recently conducted a survey of 46,000 13- to 18-year-olds—likely the biggest sample in U.S. history—to mark its centennial. The organization's *Youth Report to America*, published in March 2006, states that 48 percent of American teens said their parents and guardians "significantly influence their decisions." Dr. Alvin F. Poussaint, professor of psychiatry at Harvard Medical School, said of the study, "Youth value the opinions of their adult mentors, especially their parents' opinion."

Keeping an open line of communication shouldn't happen just during special times when you and your kids sit down to talk about Internet safety; it's about your entire relationship. How you talk with your kids about everything, your interest in their activities, and conversations over dinner are all part of how we parents help our children grow into adults. At the end of the day, Internet safety isn't about rules; it's about critical thinking skills. Children need to learn to think for themselves—to protect themselves and to internalize those values that will help transform them into safe, careful, and caring adults.

In addition to communicating openly with your kids, we recommend sharing some online guidelines. "Safe Blogging Tips for Teens" (from BlogSafety.com) lists six guidelines (see the sidebar). If you want to keep things really simple, make sure your teens are aware of the two cardinal rules of online safety:

- Never reveal personally identifiable information, such as your name, address, or phone number (including your cell phone number).

- Be extremely careful about face-to-face meetings with people you meet online.

BlogSafety.com also offers social-networking tips for parents (see the sidebar on Page 134).

Safe Blogging Tips for Teens

(from BlogSafety.com)

Be as anonymous as possible. Avoid posting information that could enable a stranger to locate you. That information includes your last name, the name of your school, local sports teams, the town you live in, and where you hang out.

Protect your information. Check to see whether your service has a friends list that allows you to control who can visit your profile or blog. If so, allow only people you know and trust. If you don't use privacy features, anyone can see your information, including people with bad intentions.

Avoid in-person meetings. Don't get together with someone you "meet" in a profile or blog unless you are certain of his or her actual identity. Although it's still not risk free, if you do meet the person, arrange the meeting in a public place, and bring some friends along.

Photos: Think before posting. What's uploaded to the Net can be downloaded by anyone and passed around or posted online pretty much forever. Avoid posting photos that allow people to identify you (for example, when they're searching for your high school), especially sexually suggestive images. Before uploading a photo, think about how you'd feel if it were seen by a parent or grandparent, college admissions counselor, or future employer.

Check comments regularly. If you allow comments on your profile or blog, check them often. Don't respond to mean or embarrassing comments. Delete them, and if possible, block offensive people from commenting further.

Be honest about your age. Membership rules exist to protect people. If you are too young to sign up, do not attempt to lie about your age. Talk with your parents about alternative sites that may be appropriate for you.

Social-Networking Tips for Parents

(from BlogSafety.com)

In addition to laying down some guidelines for kids, we also have some tips for parents:

- **Be reasonable, and try to set reasonable expectations.** Pulling the plug on children's Internet activities is rarely a good first response to a problem; it's too easy for them to go underground and establish free messaging and social-networking accounts at a friend's house or many other places.

- **Be open with your teens,** and encourage them to come to you if they encounter a problem online. Cultivate trust and communication; no rules, laws, or filtering software can replace you as their first line of defense. Teaching your kids to be critical thinkers about their safety will pay dividends for years to come.

- **Talk with your kids** about how they use the services. Make sure that they understand basic Internet and social-networking safety guidelines. These include protecting privacy (including passwords), never posting personally identifying information, avoiding in-person meetings with people they meet online, and not posting inappropriate or potentially embarrassing photos. Suggest that they use the services' privacy tools to share information only with people they know from the real world and that they never admit "friends" to their pages unless they are certain who those people are.

- **Consider requiring that all online activity take place in a central area of the home,** not in a kid's bedroom. Be aware that there are also ways kids can access the Internet away from home, including on many phones, game players, and other portable devices.

- **Try to get your kids to share their blogs or online profiles with you,** but be aware that they can have multiple accounts on multiple services. Use search engines and the search tools on social-networking sites to search for your child's full name, phone number, and other identifying information.

Privacy Options for Older Teens

As we explained earlier, MySpace now allows all users to create a private profile that can been viewed by only their friends. Users who are 16 years or older by default have public profiles, so if you have older teens, there's a good chance that their profiles are public. We suggest that parents talk with their teens about the plusses and minuses of having a private profile (see "Privacy Is a Double-Edge Sword" in Chapter 5).

Reporting Misconduct on MySpace

If you're on someone's profile and see something that you consider to be inappropriate, you can report it to MySpace right from that page by clicking the Report Inappropriate Content link at the bottom of that page (**FIGURE 6.1**). The link takes you to a page where you can send an email to customer service.

About | FAQ | Terms | Privacy | Safety Tips | Contact MySpace | Report Inappropriate Content | Promote! | Advertise | MySpace International

FIGURE 6.1 To send a report to MySpace, click the Report Inappropriate Content link at the bottom of the person's profile. Click the Terms link to see what the site defines as inappropriate.

KEY PARENTING POINT

Inappropriate content comprises anything that violates MySpace's terms of use, which are spelled out on the site's Terms page. (To access that page, click the Terms link located at the bottom of most pages—see Figure 6.1). This type of content includes nudity or postings that are "excessively violent, harassing, sexually explicit or otherwise objectionable."

In addition to inappropriate content on people's profiles, there are other forms of misconduct that you should consider reporting, such as spam, underage users, cyberbullying, copyright violation, or anything else that you feel violates MySpace terms.

You can report misconduct by using the Contact MySpace link at the bottom of every page.

Follow these steps:

1. Click the Contact MySpace link (**FIGURE 6.2**).

About | FAQ | Terms | Privacy | Safety Tips | Contact MySpace | Promote! | Advertise | MySpace International
©2003-2006 MySpace.com. All Rights Reserved.

FIGURE 6.2 Click Contact MySpace if you have a comment, question, or report to send the service.

The page that displays has two boxes at the top, one linking to the site's latest updates, and the other to the MySpace FAQ (**FIGURE 6.3**). MySpace really hopes you'll try to find what you're looking for before you send them email. You can look at the FAQ, but if you're writing about an abuse issue, it's not going to solve your problem.

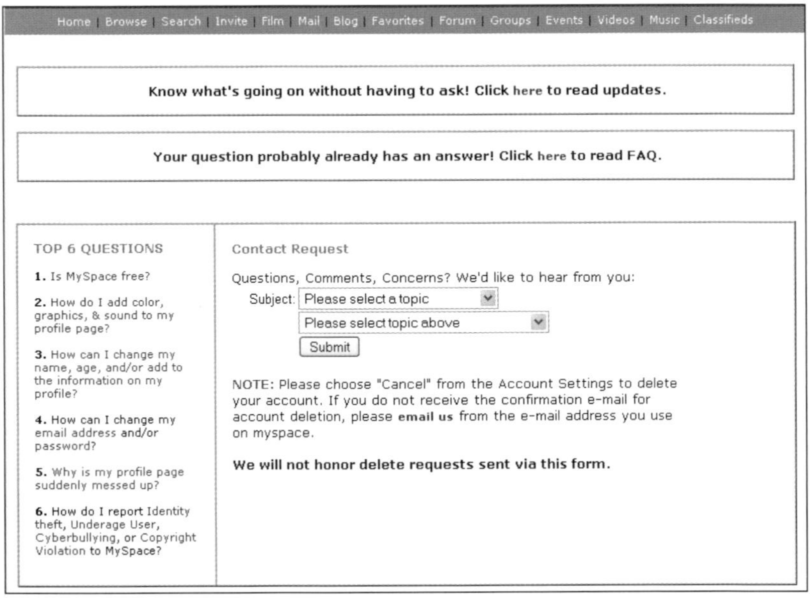

Home | Browse | Search | Invite | Film | Mail | Blog | Favorites | Forum | Groups | Events | Videos | Music | Classifieds

Know what's going on without having to ask! Click here to read updates.

Your question probably already has an answer! Click here to read FAQ.

TOP 6 QUESTIONS

1. Is MySpace free?

2. How do I add color, graphics, & sound to my profile page?

3. How can I change my name, age, and/or add to the information on my profile?

4. How can I change my email address and/or password?

5. Why is my profile page suddenly messed up?

6. How do I report Identity theft, Underage User, Cyberbullying, or Copyright Violation to MySpace?

Contact Request

Questions, Comments, Concerns? We'd like to hear from you:

Subject: [Please select a topic ▼]

[Please select topic above ▼]

[Submit]

NOTE: Please choose "Cancel" from the Account Settings to delete your account. If you do not receive the confirmation e-mail for account deletion, please **email us** from the e-mail address you use on myspace.

We will not honor delete requests sent via this form.

FIGURE 6.3 You can send a report to MySpace using the Contact Request box.

2. Click the arrow beside the Subject field. When the list of topics displays, you'll probably want to select Reporting Abuse (**FIGURE 6.4**). Then click the Please Select a Subtopic message that pops up and click Submit.

A Preliminary Response to Question screen displays links to answers to commonly asked questions.

Contact Request

Questions, Comments, Concerns? We'd like to hear from you:

     Subject: Reporting Abuse ⌄

                Cyberbullying ⌄

                [Submit]

NOTE: Please choose "Cancel" from the Account Settings to delete your account. If you do not receive the confirmation e-mail for account deletion, please **email us** from the e-mail address you use on myspace.

We will not honor delete requests sent via this form.

FIGURE 6.4 The pull-down menus require you to select a topic, and then a subtopic.

3. Assuming you still want to send the message, click No, Email Customer Service (**FIGURE 6.5**).

Home | Browse | Search | Invite | Film | Mail | Blog | Favorites | Forum | Groups | Events | Videos | Music | Classifieds

Preliminary Response to Question
The FAQs below may be relevant to your question:

- Someone on MySpace is bugging/harrassing/threatening me – what can I do about it?
- How do I block a user?
- How do we remove a teacher/faculty member's false profile?
- I think someone compromised my account, I can't log in, and things look different!

Does this answer your question?

[Yes, Exit] [No, Email Customer Service]

FIGURE 6.5 At last you can actually send your message.

4. Finally, you get to a page where you can type your note. If you're logged into MySpace, your name and email address are probably already there. If not, type them in, type your message in the Message box and click Submit Question (**FIGURE 6.6**).

KEY PARENTING POINT

If you are reporting what you believe to be a crime, or if there is any risk to life, property, or safety, contact your local police department as well. If it's a case of sexual exploitation of a child or suspected child pornography, contact the CyberTipline at www.cybertipline.com or call 800-843-5678.

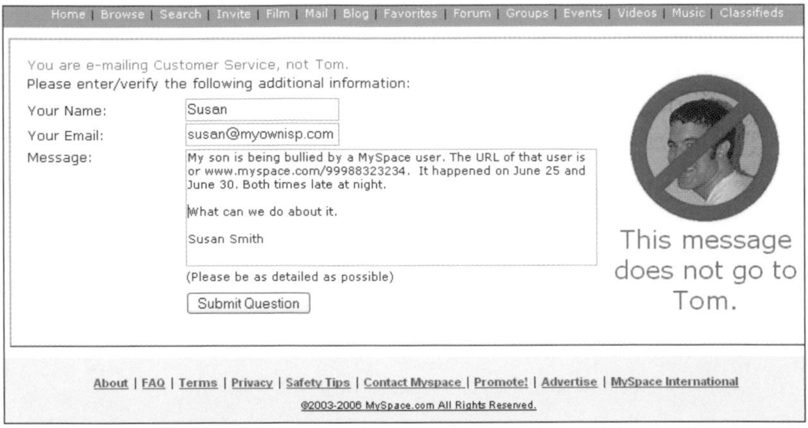

Home | Browse | Search | Invite | Film | Mail | Blog | Favorites | Forum | Groups | Events | Videos | Music | Classifieds

You are e-mailing Customer Service, not Tom.
Please enter/verify the following additional information:

Your Name: Susan

Your Email: susan@myownisp.com

Message:

My son is being bullied by a MySpace user. The URL of that user is
or www.myspace.com/99988323234. It happened on June 25 and
June 30. Both times late at night.

What can we do about it.

Susan Smith

(Please be as detailed as possible)

[Submit Question]

This message
does not go to
Tom.

About | FAQ | Terms | Privacy | Safety Tips | Contact Myspace | Promote! | Advertise | MySpace International

©2003-2006 MySpace.com All Rights Reserved.

FIGURE 6.6 Type your message to MySpace Customer Care staff.

Use Our BlogSafety Forum

We maintain an interactive forum at BlogSafety.com where you can
ask questions and interact with others. Although the forum is not
a hotline or a watchdog organization, in many cases, you can get
answers very quickly from us, other experts, or other parents—who are
often the best experts around! If you report a serious problem on the
forum, we will do our best to bring it to the attention of MySpace officials or advise you as to what we think you should do (**FIGURE 6.7**).

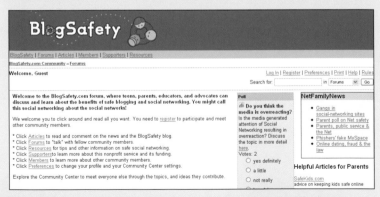

FIGURE 6.7 Now, at BlogSafety.com, there's a place to talk about
online-safety and parenting issues with experts and fellow parents.

Finding Your Child Online

The ideal way to monitor your child's site is to visit it often and look around. If your child has a private profile, have him or her add you as a friend so you can check in every now and then. Ask for the URL (Web address) of your teen's page. If your child doesn't give you that information, you may still be able to find it.

Searching for Your Child's Profile

If your child has a public profile, you—or anyone—can find his or her MySpace site, provided you know what to look for.

To access the MySpace search feature, follow these steps:

1. On any page in the site, click Search on the blue navigation bar at the top of the page. On the MySpace.com home page, you can also use the Search box on the right. If you use the Search box, first select the MySpace radio button under the text box, so you'll be searching only MySpace and not the entire Web (**FIGURE 6.8**).

FIGURE 6.8 Make sure you're just searching MySpace (if you're looking for a profile on it) by selecting the MySpace radio button, and then type your child's info into the Search field.

2. Type your child's name, email address, or what you think might be the display name or screen name (a kind of nickname) in the Search field, and then select either The Web or MySpace radio buttons beneath the Search field to indicate the parameters of your search (**FIGURE 6.9**).

TIP

In some cases, you may need to be a MySpace member to access information. If so, go ahead and sign up for a free account; you don't have to put any info in it.

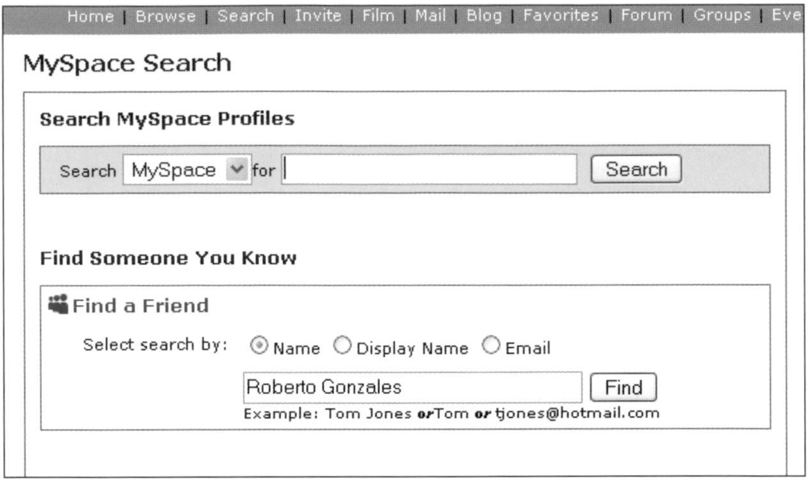

FIGURE 6.9 MySpace search works like most Web search engines.

If the information you're searching for appears in your child's profile, you'll see a page where you can view the profile, if it's public, by clicking View Profile. If the profile is private, you will see some information but not the full profile (**FIGURE 6.10**).

FIGURE 6.10 If your child's profile displays and is public, you can click on the blue "View Profile" link on the right to see what the rest of the world can see.

It is quite possible for your child to sign up under a different name, of course, or from an email address you may not be aware of (**FIGURE 6.11**). Some teens might decide to tell only certain friends their fictitious name or URL and "stealth" email address or IM screen name, and it'd be tough

FIGURE 6.11 This fictitious 14-year-old, "Susie," has a private profile, but anyone can see her first name, gender, age, sexual orientation, location, and the fact she's "here for" dating. If she had posted a photo, it too would be displayed.

for anyone else to find the profile. Anyone can get free email addresses and IM accounts from services like Hotmail, AIM, and Yahoo!.

You can also try searching MySpace, Google, and other search engines for other information, such as your child's cell phone number, street address, screen name, friends' names, school name, sports team names, or anything else that might show up on the Web or in a profile.

Browsing by School

Another way a parent might search for a son or daughter is to use the Classmate Finder option in MySpace's search area (**FIGURE 6.12**).

To use this option:

1. Type the school name in the Classmate Finder search box and also indicate the school's country and state.

2. When you find the school among your search results, you can narrow your search for your child by gender, age range, and whether your child is a current student or a graduate. You can also enter optional key words (the names of clubs or teams he's a member of) on the right side (**FIGURE 6.13**).

Because some kids lie about their ages, it's best to choose an age range—for example, from 16 to 100 (a lot of teens are pretty random about their "ages"—many just say "100").

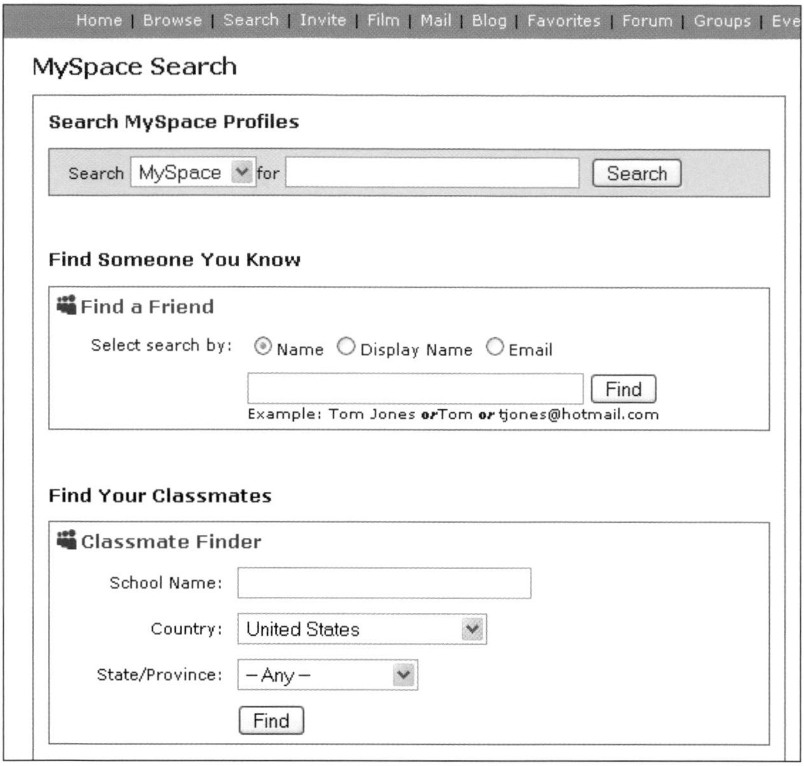

FIGURE 6.12 Type your child's school name and other info into Classmate Finder.

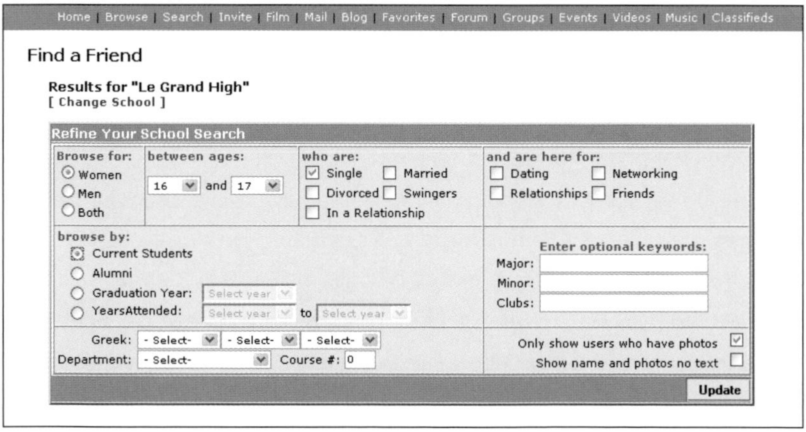

FIGURE 6.13 Provide the search tool with as much info as you can think of to refine your search.

Alternatives for 'Tweens

MySpace personnel and site-monitoring technology do look for profiles of kids who appear to be younger than 14, and if they find or receive reports about those profiles, the profiles are deleted. But MySpace staff can't find all of those profiles, and a user whose profile is deleted can just create a new one. If you discover that your child under 14 has a MySpace profile, you can request that it be canceled. But along with doing that, consider helping your child find another outlet for socializing that's more age-appropriate. For example, Imbee.com is a new social-networking site for kids 8 to 14 that includes parental controls, and AOL has a number of kids-only and teens-only services and forums for its paid members (**FIGURE 6.14**).

FIGURE 6.14 Tweens from 8 to 14 years old can socialize online with a little more supervision at Imbee.com.

Monitoring and Filtering

Because of concerns about MySpace, more and more parental-controls software companies are adding social-networking monitoring to either their products or their marketing of these products, and new MySpace-specific products are coming on the market. The line-up is changing fast, so for a comprehensive view of what's available, you'll need to do a product search in a Web search engine to get product ads or a list of search results. Search using phrases like "monitor MySpace," "blog monitoring," or "MySpace parental controls."

Monitoring Services

The most useful thing about the MySpace-specific services is that they alert you to changes to your child's profile, assuming that the profile is public.

KEY PARENTING POINT

There is an important difference between services that monitor changes to your child's public profile and monitoring software that records everything your kids do on the PC. The former is simply a convenient way for you to see what anyone else can see—what your kid is posting in public. PC monitoring software can be used to spy on everything your child types and sees, including private messages.

MySpaceWatch.com, which is not affiliated with MySpace, offers both a free and a fee-based service to help you track what's happening in your kids' profiles. The free version will monitor one profile and crawl (look for updates) twice a day. The $6-per-month version monitors up to five profiles and provides a list of your child's friends and updates every 6 hours (**FIGURE 6.15**).

Services like this provide limited information, but they do make it easy to get updates, assuming that your child is registered under his or her real name or an email address you know about. There is also the possibility that you're spending a lot of time monitoring only *one* of your child's accounts, and it may even be the one he or she intended you to see. That kids can establish multiple accounts on multiple services is a distinct limitation of these products. They can give you a false sense of security.

As of this writing, MySpaceWatch was still available, but another similar service, KidQuery, folded as we went to press. In a June 29, 2006, article "Keeping an Eye on MySpace," CNET's Stefanie Olsen reported that KidQuery "closed after one of the engineers realized it could violate the terms of service of MySpace, which restricts other services from crawling and lifting data from its network."

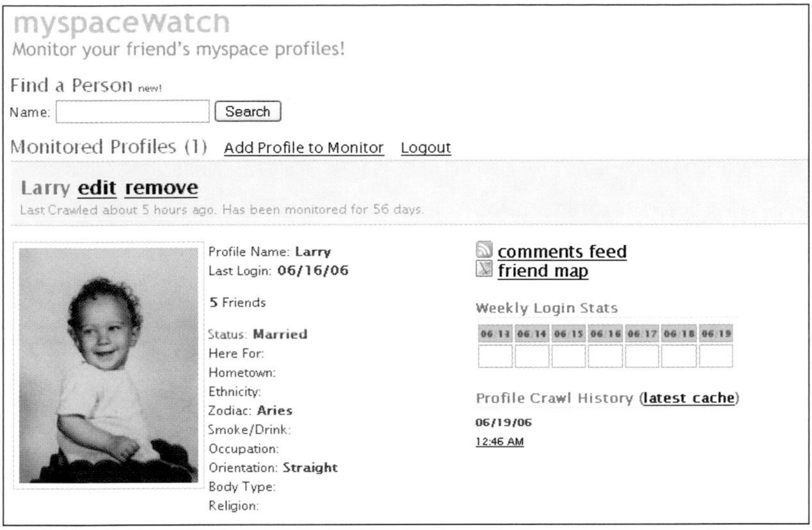

myspaceWatch
Monitor your friend's myspace profiles!

Find a Person new!
Name: [   ]   [Search]

Monitored Profiles (1)   Add Profile to Monitor   Logout

Larry edit remove
Last Crawled about 5 hours ago. Has been monitored for 56 days.

Profile Name: **Larry**
Last Login: **06/16/06**

5 Friends

Status: **Married**
Here For:
Hometown:
Ethnicity:
Zodiac: **Aries**
Smoke/Drink:
Occupation:
Orientation: **Straight**
Body Type:
Religion:

comments feed
friend map

Weekly Login Stats

06 13 06 14 06 15 06 16 06 17 06 18 06 19

Profile Crawl History (**latest cache**)
06/19/06
12:46 AM

FIGURE 6.15 The paid version of myspaceWatch lets you view a summary of your child's profile, get updates on comments, and see who your child's "friends" are.

Monitoring Software

Monitoring software can log and report to you everything your child is doing on that particular computer—all the keystrokes, whether in IM or email, on social networks or other Web sites, or in word-processing and other programs.

One problem with monitoring software is that, like filters, they can't be everywhere; they work only on the machine where they're installed. As the Internet becomes available in more and more places and on growing numbers of portable devices, "parental controls" software is getting less helpful.

An even greater potential problem is that monitoring can lead to distrust if your kid knows or suspects you are "spying" on everything happening on the PC. We're not here to judge the choice you make. All parents need to do what's appropriate for their families, but we urge you to be very thoughtful before installing monitoring software or signing on with a monitoring service. If you do decide to use it, consider telling your kids you've installed it so that they know it's there; they might figure it out anyway.

"Tracking software presupposes a lack of trust between parent and child, and it is very difficult to go back. Indeed, this is a 'last resort' approach," wrote parent and technology educator Jeff Cooper in our BlogSafety.com forum. We agree.

If you're interested in using monitoring software, the leading provider is SpectorSoft. Another is (appropriately named?) IamBigBrother (**FIGURE 6.16**).

FIGURE 6.16 For better or worse, IamBigBrother lets you "see everything your family is doing online."

Filtering

Numerous programs are available that are designed to *filter* the Web (block kids from visiting certain types of sites on your home computer).

Software like CYBERsitter, Net Nanny, CyberPatrol, and Norton Parental Controls generally do a good job of keeping kids away from porn, hateful messages, and other areas of the Web that parents want to keep off limits. You can also configure most of these programs to add or remove sites, so it's possible to use one of these programs to keep your kids from visiting MySpace (and many are adding social networking to their lists of blocked sites).

As you might have guessed, we don't recommend that you filter out social-networking sites, especially for teenagers, for several reasons:

- All you would accomplish would be to block your children on the computer at home. Filters will do nothing to keep them from visiting the sites on other computers or on cell phones or other devices.

- Although these filters can be effective in keeping small children from visiting certain types of sites accidentally, they are pretty lame when it comes to computer-savvy teens who can probably find a way around them. Plenty of proxy sites help in-the-know teens bypass any filters that their parents or schools put on a computer or network. Sites like UnblockMe and HideUS (and there are many more) allow users to go anywhere they want, despite filters and without detection.

- As we've mentioned several times throughout this book, even if you could keep teens from using MySpace, you might wind up driving them to other, less accountable or more dangerous sites, in effect encouraging them to go underground for their social networking.

Canceling Your Child's Account

If you feel you must cancel your child's MySpace account, that is certainly your right as a parent. However, the only easy way to do that is with your child's cooperation.

In its Frequently Asked Questions, MySpace suggests, "Please work with your child to remove the account." That advice may seem to be unhelpful, but cooperation is important. Even if your child does agree to remove his profile, there is nothing to stop him from setting up a new profile that might be even harder for you to find—or setting up an account on another social-networking service.

The Email Issue

Sometimes, kids set up accounts by using a fake email address. If the child is cooperative, and you've followed the basic account-cancellation steps but haven't received the confirmation email that's supposed to come within 24 hours, log into the child's profile and delete all the information in it (Headline, About Me, Interests, and so on). Then type in one of those boxes, "Remove this profile."

Next, send an email to CustomerCare@MySpace.com. In that email, provide the URL (Web address) of your child's account, such as www. myspace.com/susiemsith or www.myspace.com/99999999. (The URL is displayed in the My URL box of the user's home page, just below the Hello box.)

Next in your email, state that you want the profile to be removed and that the profile is now blank except for the instruction to remove it.

Without Your Child's Help

If you can't get into the account, send an email to "DeleteAccount@ MySpace.com" with the profile's URL and ask that the profile be deleted. Without that URL, MySpace has no way of knowing which of the millions of profiles belongs to your child. If you don't know the address, try searching for it in MySpace's search box, using information such as your child's first and last names, school name, friends' URLs or names, as we describe in "Finding Your Child Online," earlier in this chapter. If there's evidence in the profile that the child is younger than MySpace's minimum age of 14, MySpace will delete the account—usually, within 48 hours of verification. In any case, you will receive an automated email providing a number that you can call to discuss your case.

Impersonators

If you can't get into the account because someone else created it to imper-sonate, embarrass, or otherwise harass your child, MySpace says, "We remove it on sight." Just email customer care@myspace.com to request deletion, again with the URL or address of the profile.

But keep in mind that realistically, there aren't enough hours in a day, week, or month in parents' schedules to find and, if desired, take down every account their kids have established online. It's better to work with your children on safe online socializing than to ban it and, in the process, send them into stealth mode. Open MySpace use, with ground rules, is much safer!

Your Best Defense. . .

While you may be heartened to learn of all the tools available to help keep kids safe on MySpace, remember what we said at the start of the chapter: Your best tool is maintaining an open relationship with your kids.

And here's another piece of advice you probably didn't expect to find in a book about MySpace: One way to help your kids stay safe online is to have meals together as a family. We all lead busy lives, and it's very easy to just grab food on our own. But family dinners are a chance to talk, process your day, and just be together. We're not suggesting that you talk about MySpace at dinner (lest you choke on your food), just that you spend time together and take interest in each other's lives. It's what relationships—and parenting—are all about.

CHAPTER 7

MySpacers' Advanced Tricks and Tips

TRICKS FOR CUSTOMIZING MYSPACE may seem a bit much to many parents, but millions of kids are customizing and doing a whole lot more to their spaces. That kids should want to use tools to spiff up their pages should come as no surprise. MySpace profiles aren't just Web sites, as we mentioned in Chapter 2. They're one avenue kids use to express themselves, show off, make friends, one-up their friends, and create and recreate their online identities.

We don't expect many parents will want to implement the tricks featured in this chapter. But by reading through it you'll get a good idea of what a lot of kids are doing. Maybe you'll even discover a trick or two you can pass on to your kids and score a point or two!

Pimping and Hacking: Oh My!

A common phrase related to customizing that MySpace users like to throw around is "Pimp Your MySpace." We're not exactly thrilled by the choice of words, since "pimp" is a term associated with the exploitation of women. Even so, and thanks largely to the popular TV show "Pimp My Ride," the term has taken on a new connotation that means something like "customize," but it's really more than that. It's the process of personalizing one's space so that it's not just unique but pretty flashy.

Another word you might have heard teens use a lot is "hacks." Though the term "hacker" is commonly used to describe criminals who break into computer systems, it's also a term of endearment used to describe savvy computer users who figure out clever ways to make products and Web sites do incredible things. There are plenty of "MySpace hacks" that allow users to customize their pages. So as offensive as "pimp" is to some and "hacks" to others, in the world of MySpace they are seen by many as good things than can bring extra status to those who master them.

HTML Is Key

Not all MySpace customizations are designed to make the pages flashier. Once you delve into this world, you'll find all sorts of things you can do to transform MySpace into your space.

The key to being able to modify MySpace beyond the features available from the service itself is that MySpace makes it possible to embed computer code called "HTML" (HyperText Markup Language) directly into certain parts of a user profile. With this code, users can do almost anything any Web designer could do, including change the background colors, add more pictures or videos, display animation, or link out to media or material on other Web sites.

HTML code looks a little like code from any programming language, and some tech-savvy MySpace users have taken the time to actually learn how to program in HTML, so that they can have a great deal of control over how their MySpace profile looks and works (**FIGURE 7.1**). But you don't really need to know anything about HTML to use it. That's because there are numerous Web sites that will automatically generate the code for you. All you have to do is copy it onto your Windows or Mac clipboard, point to the appropriate spot on your MySpace profile, and paste it in. Still, a little HTML knowledge goes a long way and will allow you to get the most out of the experience. We think that's a good thing, because it encourages teens to study HTML, which teaches them about Web design and computer programming, two skills that can be very useful for their futures.

```
<form action='http://www.kwiz.biz/simplesurveys/do-
survey.php' method='post' target='_new'><table border=1
bordercolor=#efefef cellspacing=0><tr><td valign=top
align=center colspan=2><b><i>TELL ME ABOUT YOURSELF - The
Survey</i></b><input type='hidden' name='question1'
value='TELL+ME+ABOUT+YOURSELF+-+The+Survey'><input
type='hidden' name='type1' value='2'></td
></tr><tr><td valign=top
```

FIGURE 7.1 Some (not all) HTML code is pretty hard to decipher, but it's definitely not rocket science, and there are lots of Web sites that will generate it for you.

Before You Customize

There are a couple of downsides to the ability to customize MySpace.

First, while a few choice profile customizations can make a profile more personal and cool, too much stuff can look cluttered or gaudy, or make it difficult for others to navigate your page. They could even keep a profile from functioning at all.

Second, poorly constructed custom MySpace profiles can freeze up your Web browser because of improper coding or excessive design elements. This is especially true when high-bandwidth items such as Flash animations, videos, and music are added.

Third, customization can sometimes bring up some safety and computer-security issues. For example, some MySpacers like to fill out third-party surveys and post the results on their page, as we mentioned in Chapter 5. Some of these surveys encourage people to answer questions like "Have you gone skinny dipping?" or "Have you stolen anything?" or "Have you ever been drunk?" Some even ask questions of a sexual nature. The third-party sites that host the surveys often generate HTML code, based on the answers the kids provide, which MySpace users can use to post the survey results on their profiles. The downside to this technique, besides the fact that kids are posting information about themselves that's better kept private, is that when you add code from an untrusted source to a MySpace profile, you run the risk of linking out to dangerous sites that could cause security or other problems for you or your computer and for people who visit your MySpace page (**FIGURE 7.2**).

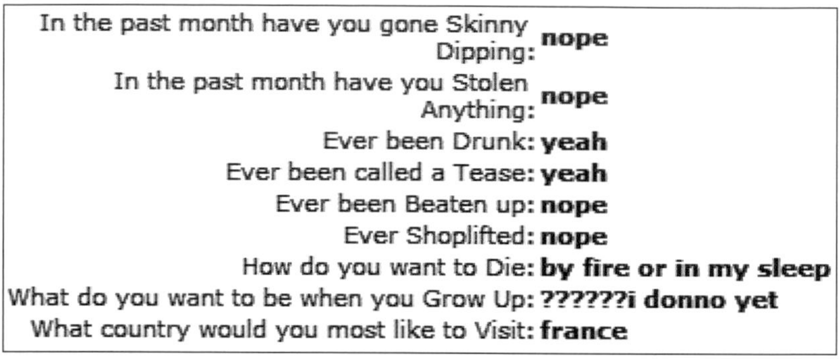

In the past month have you gone Skinny Dipping: **nope**
In the past month have you Stolen Anything: **nope**
Ever been Drunk: **yeah**
Ever been called a Tease: **yeah**
Ever been Beaten up: **nope**
Ever Shoplifted: **nope**
How do you want to Die: **by fire or in my sleep**
What do you want to be when you Grow Up: **??????i donno yet**
What country would you most like to Visit: **france**

FIGURE 7.2 A portion of one of many third-party surveys available to MySpace users.

Keeping HTML From Doing Bad Things

The good news about HTML is that what goes in can also come out. Kids who paste HTML on their profiles should look at the profile immediately to see if there are any problems. It's also a very good idea to check the profile on a regular basis to screen friends' comments, which can also contain HTML code along with text. If there are problems with code pasted into any of the fields in the Profile Edit section, you or your teen should go back to that section and remove the code, unless one of you happens to be an HTML wizard and can fix any errant code.

In addition to code that's pasted in the Profile Edit section, HTML can also be placed in photo captions, in descriptions for groups your child might moderate, and comments other people post in your child's profile. Teens need to be especially alert when it comes to code their friends include in comments. If there is a problem with that code or with any text in these sections, it can be edited using Safe Edit Mode (sometimes referred to as "Safe Mode").

To access Safe Edit Mode, follow these steps:

1. In the Hello box on your home page, click Edit Profile.

2. Click Safe Edit Mode near the upper right corner of the Profile Edit page (**FIGURE 7.3**).

FIGURE 7.3 Click on Safe Edit Mode to remove HTML code from groups, comments, or photo captions.

3. Click Groups, Comments, or Images.

4. You can delete or edit code or text in Groups and Images. You can only delete code or text in comments (**FIGURE 7.4**).

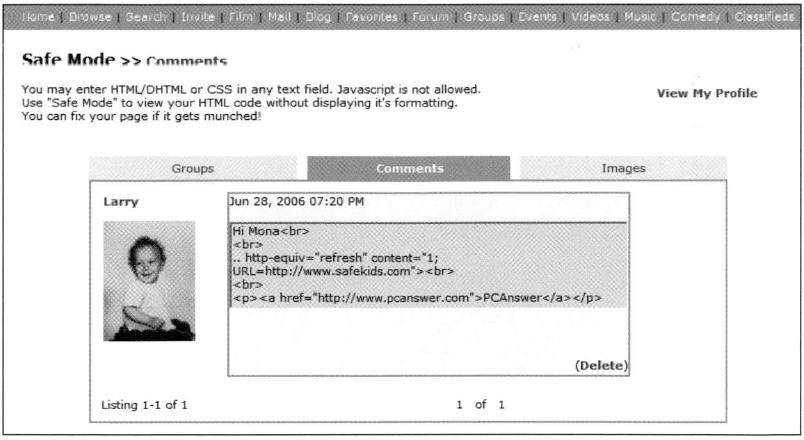

FIGURE 7.4 Safe Edit Mode lets you delete HTML code in groups, captions, and comments. Shown here is code that was entered as part of a comment by a friend.

Making Profiles Sing and Dance

It's very easy to add color, graphics, and artistic personality to a MySpace profile by pasting HTML into the appropriate places. We'll explain how to do that in a minute, but first you need to know how to find or generate the code that you want to paste in. That's where MySpace Editors come in handy.

Using MySpace Editors

There are numerous sites on the Web that offer what are called "MySpace editors." They're easy-to-use interactive templates that generate HTML code based on information you provide so that you can jazz up your standard profile.

You don't need to know anything about HTML to use MySpace editors. For example, MySpace Editor (www.myspacecode.com) offers an easy-to-use online Profile Editor that lets you pick a different background color, background image, and page border color for your profile. You can preview how the new code will affect your page. When you're finished, you click the Generate Code button, and the Web site creates the HTML code, which you simply copy to the clipboard and paste in any of the fields in the Interests and Personality section of your profile (**FIGURE 7.5**).

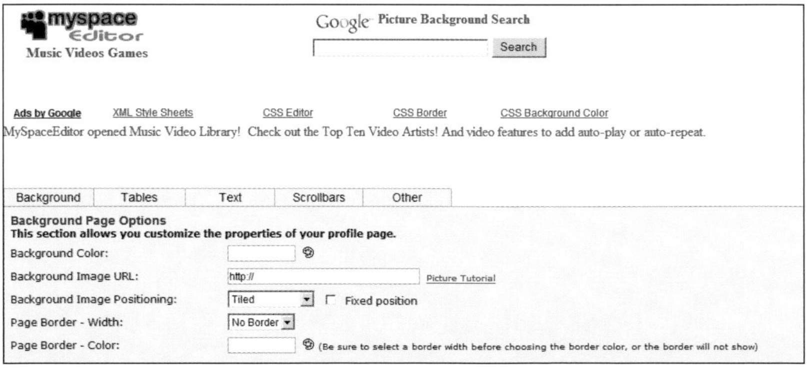

FIGURE 7.5 One of the many sites that generate code for spiffing up profiles, mySpace Editor is free and easy to use.

Use Caution When Visiting Customization Sites

Many of the sites that provide customization codes make money through advertising, so it's not uncommon to get pop-ups and other obnoxious ads when you visit these sites. We can't vouch for the integrity of these sites, so if you visit them, use caution about providing any personal information. Keep in mind, too, that third-party sites like these tend to come and go, based on economics, as well as the legality of their business practices.

There are plenty of other online editors that you can use, including Thomas' MySpace Editor (http://206.225.92.10/myspace/) and, as you might expect, one called PimpMySpace (www.pimpmyspace.org) (**FIGURE 7.6**). You can find more in the link list at www.myspace-editors.com or by typing "MySpace editors" into any search engine.

FIGURE 7.6 PimpMySpace.org bills itself as the place for the "ultimate profile pimpin' solutions."

Pasting Code Into MySpace

You can paste the HTML code into several of the blank fields on the Profile Edit page. These fields are normally used by MySpace users to type in things like bios, favorite movies, or people they would like to meet. But they can also be used to hold HTML code that will automatically be executed when people visit your profile. The fields in which the code can be placed include About Me, I'd Like to Meet, Interests, Music, Books, Movies, Television, and Heroes.

To place the code:

1. Copy the code from a MySpace editor or other source onto the clipboard.

2. From the Hello box of your MySpace home page, click Edit Profile.

3. Place your cursor into a field such as About Me or I'd Like to Meet and paste the code into the box. If there is already code or text in that field, you can add the code at the bottom (**FIGURE 7.7**).

```
About Me:   color:; font-weight:normal;}.orangetext15{color:;
            font-weight:normal;}.lightbluetext8{font-size:8pt; color:;
            font-weight:normal;}.tmz_imp{font-family:arial;color:FF0000;
            img{}a:hover
            img{}body{scrollbar-arrow-color:;scrollbar-Track-Color:00CC9
            style='display:none' src='' AUTOSTART='True' LOOP='1'>This
            profile was edited with <a
            href='http://www.myspacehelp.net'>MySpace Help - Profile
            Creator and Editor</A><div style="width: 88px; height:
            35px; position: absolute; top:0px;left:0px;
            background-color: DEE6EB;
            border-width:1px;border-style:solid;border-color: 9CB3C3;
            font-family: Arial Black;"><a
            href="http://www.myspacehelp.net" style="color: 9CB3C3;
            font-size: 12px; position: absolute; left: 13px; top:
```

                                            Preview Section   Preview Profile

FIGURE 7.7 Pasting HTML code like this into the About Me or other text box of Profile Editor can change the look of your profile.

4. Click Preview Section to see what the HTML code does to your profile (**FIGURE 7.8**).

5. If you're happy with the change, scroll down to the bottom of the screen and click Save All Changes.

6. If you made a mistake or want to change anything, repeat the process to either remove or replace the code.

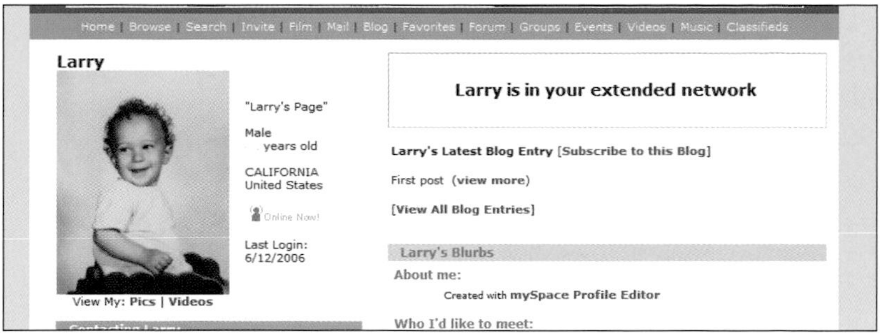

FIGURE 7.8 Larry's site with modified colors from mySpace Profile Editor. And, yes, that really is Larry!

Hotlinking

Hotlinking is a practice in which someone uses images or media files from another Web site by linking to them, rather than loading them on their own MySpace profile or using a hosting service (**FIGURE 7.9**). Because hotlinking is easier than uploading files to an appropriate server, MySpacers regularly use it, though it's not always legal. If the images or files that are being hotlinked are copyrighted and the borrower hasn't received authorization to use them, hotlinking boils down to stealing.

```
<img scr="picture.jpg" height="400" width="225"
```

FIGURE 7.9 One line of HTML code is all it takes to hotlink an image from someone else's site. Easy, but not always legal.

But that's not the only problem. Hotlinking also uses a lot of bandwidth, so the owner of the Web site hosting the files could potentially lose visitors if the site seems too slow because of the drain that hotlinking causes.

Another downside is that hotlinking can backfire because you have no control over the source location. If the other site goes down or is running slowly, your image won't show up. And if the webmaster of that other site changes or removes the image at any time, it will affect the link to your MySpace profile and ultimately what shows up.

To counteract rampant hotlinking that infringes on their bandwidth and intellectual property, mischievous webmasters have been known to replace original hotlinked images with others (advertisements, junk, or random posts) to discourage people from stealing their images. A malicious webmaster might even do worse and put a totally inappropriate or potentially embarrassing picture or comment in its place.

Because some MySpace users were in the process of linking out to photos and other media that violated the site's Terms of Use (pornographic images, for example), MySpace had to staff up. "We are now [as of spring 2006] reviewing every single image hotlinked to our site," a MySpace customer care staffer told us.

While conducting research for this book, we came across a discussion in a graphic artists' forum about MySpace, hotlinking, and artists' concerns about intellectual property. One artist admitted to renaming linked files so that they don't appear on MySpace users' pages anymore and, in its place, creating a new file with the old name that says, "This [expletive deleted] is hotlinking a file without permission."

Linking Out From MySpace

Linking out from MySpace is different from hotlinking, and in most cases it's OK. Linking involves placing a link on a Web page—in this case a MySpace profile—that takes visitors to another Web site.

As a courtesy, it's a good idea to seek permission from the site that's being linked to. But sometimes, if it's a large site, it's not practical. With very few exceptions, linking is both legal and ethical. Links are created by embedding a small amount of HTML code in a MySpace profile that will allow visitors to go to that other site.

For example, if you wanted to place a link to our site, BlogSafety.com, within your profile, you would paste the following code in your About Me or other section, and that would be OK with us:
<a href="http://www.blogsafety.com">Visit BlogSafety.com</a>

Changing Top 8 Friends to Top 20

In Chapter 4 we discussed Your Top 8, the feature that lets MySpace users select eight people from their list of friends and then display them (in a certain order) on their profiles. This feature is currently the default, and no more than eight friends will appear in that space unless the user programs the page otherwise. Because the Top 8 in a way signifies a person's favorite friends, it can become a sensitive issue, since the list appears publicly on a Myspacer's profile.

Some advanced MySpace users try to avoid offending anyone by hacking their own profile to feature their Top 20 or Top 30 instead, or even to hide this section completely. One way to expand the Top 8 list is to visit MySpaceSupport.com and select Top 16 Friends List, which lets users display up to 40 top friends on their pages (**FIGURE 7.10**).

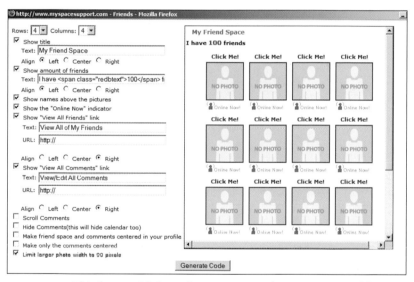

FIGURE 7.10 This form at MySpaceSupport.com makes it easy to modify a Top 8 list. If this were an active profile, you'd see real pictures, not placeholders.

Monitoring Visitors to Your Profile

There are numerous Web sites that offer tools that let you track who is visiting your page. Using a snippet of code that you post on your MySpace page, these sites track and record the MySpace users who are looking at your profile. You can find details like who, when, and what time of day they visited. Advanced spying code will even give you a link to their profiles and let you track the number of users who look at your profile over a period of a day, week, or month.

These Web tracking services are great for MySpace users who think they might have a stalker and want to monitor activity on their pages. It can also be useful for concerned parents who want to keep better tabs on who is visiting their children's pages (assuming your kids agree to post this on the page).

There's even a blog—myspacetracker.blogspot.com—that helps you keep track of all the different profile trackers (**FIGURE 7.11**).

FIGURE 7.11 A profile tracker from MySpaceReviews.com makes it easy to figure out who's been knocking on your virtual door or lurking on your profile.

Bots: Making Friends by the Thousands

In addition to being a place for friends, MySpace has also become a marketing and publicity tool. People and businesses use the site to promote their goods and services, and as MySpace continues to grow and build members, more people are making money (and even careers) out of MySpace promotion.

Automatic tools called "bots" are a big help for MySpace promoters (and often a big nuisance to everyone else) who want to target more users and extend their MySpace reach. A bot is a piece of software that interacts with Web pages—kind of like a person might, but it does it automatically. There are even companies that will mass-target MySpace users with friend requests, invitations, and more.

Bots are also used by some MySpace users to quickly build their friend base. Popular and cheap (even free) downloads for friend-generating bots are becoming more and more common. Nicknamed "Whore Trains" (ouch) or "Friend Trains," these tools help users send out massive friend requests with minimal effort (**FIGURE 7.12**).

FIGURE 7.12 A Web promotion for one of the many "bots" that can automate friend requests, etc.

Why would MySpace users want to spam a bunch of users with friend requests in hopes of adding more "friends" to their profile? Status. Publicity. Celebrity. And all those other things we talked about in Chapter 2. The My Friends space is in many ways a popularity contest, and—for some teens—the more "friends" they have, the "cooler" they are. Plus, users who've managed to build thousands of "friends" have a built-in network to advertise and promote whatever they might have going on in their lives, like music, writing, a small business, or events. MySpace is cheap advertising and an easy platform for up-and-coming somebodies from all walks of life to self promote.

Uploading Video

In Chapter 4, we wrote a bit about adding video to your profile. There are actually two ways to do that. You can use video that's already on MySpace (music videos from bands, for example) or you can upload your own video.

To search for and display on your MySpace profile a video that's already on MySpace:

1. On the blue navigation bar on any MySpace page, click Videos.

2. If you know what you're looking for, enter a search term in the text box and click Search Videos. Otherwise, browse through Top Videos or drill down into the categories via the Browse Categories tab (**FIGURE 7.13**).

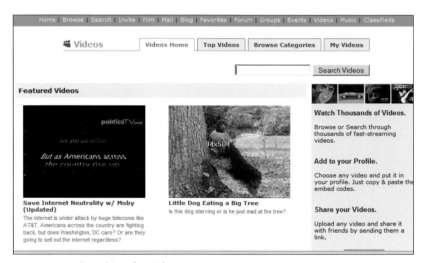

FIGURE 7.13 Searching for video.

3. When you've found a potential video, click the blue video title to view it (**FIGURE 7.14**). A media player should automatically load. (Once in a while, a computer glitch will cause media files not to play properly. If that happens, find the nearest computer expert— probably the nearest kid in your house.

4. Click the Play key on the media player to view the video.

Home | Browse | Search | Invite | Film | Mail | Blog | Favorites | Forum | Groups | Events | Videos | Music | Classifieds
Videos
Videos Home
Top Videos
Browse Categories
My Videos
Top Plays | Just Added | Most Comments | Top Rated
Show for: Today | Week | Month | All
Search Videos
Category: Animals
Listing 1-12 of 1021
1 2 3 4 5 >> of 86
Next >
Iguana Vs. Armad...
Plays: 14298 | Comments: 95
bad baby sitter
Plays: 10162 | Comments: 119
Funny Cat Jump
Plays: 8132 | Comments: 53
dumb cats
Plays: 6000 | Comments: 21

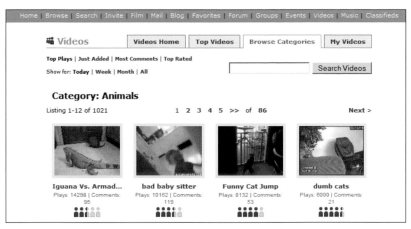

FIGURE 7.14 Select a video to display by clicking its title.

5. If you like what you see and want to include this clip on your profile, copy the code from the Video Code box on the right side of the screen.
6. Go to your MySpace home page, click Edit Profile, and paste the code into the About Me section. Then click Save All Changes. The video displays on your profile page.

To upload your own videos to the MySpace Video section:

1. On the blue navigational bar at the top of any MySpace page, click Videos.
2. Click the My Videos tab at the top of the screen, and then click Upload Video (**FIGURE 7.15**).

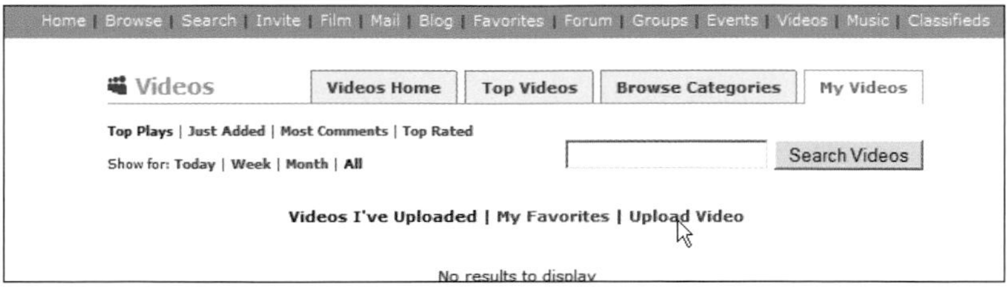

Home | Browse | Search | Invite | Film | Mail | Blog | Favorites | Forum | Groups | Events | Videos | Music | Classifieds
Videos
Videos Home
Top Videos
Browse Categories
My Videos
Top Plays | Just Added | Most Comments | Top Rated
Show for: Today | Week | Month | All
Search Videos
Videos I've Uploaded | My Favorites | Upload Video
No results to display

FIGURE 7.15 Click the "Upload Video" button to transfer video from your hard drive.

3. On the Upload Video: Step 1 page, enter a short title and description (**FIGURE 7.16**).

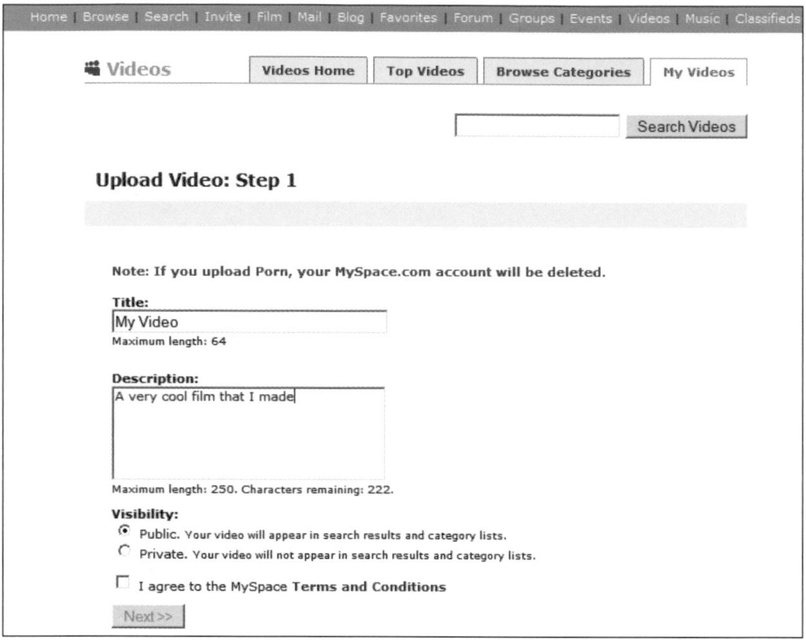

FIGURE 7.16 Name and describe your video and designate if it's public or private.

4. On the Upload Video: Step 2 page, select the appropriate categories your video falls into. You can also add tags (key words) to help people find your video.

5. On the Upload Video: Step 3 page, browse your hard drive for the video and click Upload. Video files are generally quite large, so it may take a few minutes for the process to finish.

    The video must go through MySpace approval before it appears on your profile. Photos, on the other hand, are posted automatically but reviewed by MySpace after the fact, and can be reported by other users if they're in violation of the Terms of Use.

Kids (and adults too) need to remember to consider their own privacy and the privacy of others when uploading videos (as well as photos, of course). For example, who's on display in a party video or family movie you want to upload? Have you asked their permission to be shown in a public "place"? MySpace has rules about what can and cannot be posted, including videos that contain nudity or violence or violate someone's copyright. Remind your kids that their videos could be copied and passed around long into the future.

Forums for Learning About Customizing

Another way to learn more about customizing MySpace is to use the MySpace forums, where experts offer free advice to anyone who cares to visit. As we discussed in Chapter 4, a forum is an Internet venue specifically for holding discussions (in text) and are great resources for questions, help, and advice. MySpace has a forum dedicated to all things MySpace, with both a General topic and one that focuses just on customizing. There are experts on these forums who will answer your questions. This is a great resource for finding code and learning how to do things with your profile

To browse MySpace forums:

1. Click on Forum via the blue navigational bar at the top of any MySpace screen.

2. On the Forum homepage, you'll see folders or categories with short descriptions about the forum.

3. Click on the MySpace topic and then go to either the Customizing or General subtopic. Scroll through the posts until you see one that has something interesting or addresses what you are looking for (**FIGURE 7.17**).

FIGURE 7.17 An active MySpace customizing forum where experts share their experiences.

To post a topic:

1. Click Post a Topic.

2. Enter a subject and type your question or discussion, and click Post This Topic.

3. You'll see a Preview Topic confirmation screen. Click Post This Topic to publish your comment (**FIGURE 7.18**).

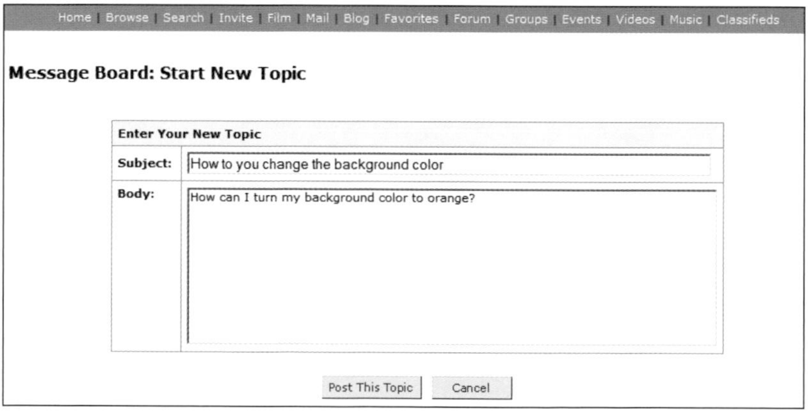

FIGURE 7.18 Posting a question on the MySpace message forum.

Now you know some of the most popular customization options that ambitious profile designers use—way more than any busy parent would want to take on. But you can at least talk intelligently about profile design with just about any teen MySpace user. And if you've created your own profile and tried out even a few of our suggestions, you're way ahead of the average parent—of most people over 30, in fact!

It's time to step away from the computer and back into your role as both a good parent and a concerned citizen. After explaining how teens use MySpace and other social networks and how you can use it and help teens make the experience safer, we're ready for the final and, ultimately, the most challenging chapter. Where do we as parents and a society go from here to make public policy that keeps pace with and encourages kids' constructive use of Web 2.0?

CHAPTER 8

Where Do We Go From Here?

A BOOK ABOUT SOCIAL networking is like suspended animation: Remember those old cartoons in which Wile E. Coyote and the Road Runner would suddenly be suspended mid-air, right at the most dramatic moment of the fastest action of the entire episode, the Coyote within millimeters of (and yet so very far from) the ultimate attainment? Of course, in the case of this book, the ultimate attainment is enough public understanding of MySpace and teen social networking to allow for just the right balance of free expression and safety.

Our challenge is that not only are MySpace, social networking, and the Web moving targets, but so is public awareness. By its very nature the user-driven Web is unpredictable. It's a *collective* product, process, experience, and experiment. So all of us are determining where the Web is headed, and ideally we're safety-trained, critically thinking participants.

But despite this inherent unpredictability, there are some things we're pretty sure about from close observation since the early days of the Web.

Teens Are in the Driver's Seat

Web 2.0 is not going away anytime soon, and it's hardly something we can control (except maybe in our own homes). In fact, the interactive, user-produced Web is driven by people under 30, according to a May 2006 Pew Internet & American Life study of broadband Internet access. The report, "Home Broadband Adoption 2006," found that "fully 51% of 'under 30' home broadband users have posted content to the Internet, compared with 36% of home high-speed users older than 30."

So the socializing or creative networking part of Web 2.0 is not only here to stay, but increasingly what the Web is all about. The Web is not just a teens' hangout, but also their storage locker, research tool, communications tool, entertainment medium, and news channel—and the distinctions between these functions are increasingly blurred.

However, here's what we *do* know:

- **Internet natives.** Our kids are the "digital natives," or those who have not known life without the Internet. And we "digital immigrants" need to interact—to learn *as* we teach media literacy and online safety—so we can effectively parent our Net-fluent children.

- **Influence vs. control.** The more we try to control a user-driven medium like Web 2.0, the more workarounds its producers find—whether we're talking about laws or parenting. In this media environment, it's the responsible Web sites and obedient kids who are reached by the rules, not the irresponsible or defiant ones. Some fresh thinking, parenting, and governing are needed if we want to influence the latter.

- **A blurred distinction.** More and more of our kids' lives are either online or mirrored online, as the distinction between online and offline continues to fade in their minds.

- **A healthy skepticism.** The need for critical thinking about whom we're interacting with and what we're consuming and expressing is only growing—for all of us—because so much is done in public and can be recorded forever.

- **Identity play.** Wherever anonymity is allowed—wherever IDs can't be confirmed—teens will play with identity by trying on different personas, which is usually, but not always, constructive.

- **Support risk asssessment.** Teens experiment and take risks in the process of learning who they are socially, emotionally, and physically, and we do them a disservice if we don't let them or if we try to remove all risk.

- **Uploading too.** On Web 2.0, parents need to be concerned not only with inappropriate material that kids "download," but personal information and material that they "upload."

- **Perspective needed.** We need to put risks into context. While there are dangers in social networking, children face a far greater danger from people they already know. Do we ban school, religious and family gatherings because of the risk of predators in those venues, or do we teach our kids critical thinking skills that can protect them online and offline?

- **Life literacy/tech literacy.** Remember "Parental guidance suggested." Transfer all that good parenting sense you already have into cyberspace. Don't worry if you don't have your kids' level of tech literacy—they can help you with that. They need your guidance on life literacy.

- **Interactive solution development.** It's OK that parents don't have all the answers. Schools, lawmakers, and law-enforcement people don't either. Nor do we, of course. Not having all the answers forces us all to talk about social networking—in our homes, schools, and communities. This interdependence is a good thing because on a user-driven, social Web, the solutions need to be collective, interactive, and evolving too.

Parents in the Car

Just as teen drivers in training need an experienced driver in the car, parents need to be "in the car" where teens' online social lives are concerned. In the same way that we ask them, "Who are you going out with tonight?"

or "Who else is going to the concert or party?" we also need to ask them who they're spending time with online.

Remember that it doesn't help a student driver to have someone in the car who is petrified by teen fatality statistics and has buried the keys in the backyard. It just helps to have someone in the side seat, offering guidance and pointers along the way.

There Ought to Be a Law. . .

Just before we put this book to bed, we took a couple of days to travel to Washington, D.C., to help moderate a one-day conference on social-networking safety sponsored by the National Center for Missing & Exploited Children. Panelists included law enforcement leaders, leading pediatricians, online safety experts, the Attorneys General of Connecticut and North Carolina, the CEO of Xanga, the Chief Privacy Office of Facebook and, for this first public appearance since taking the job, Hemanshu Nigam, the chief security officer for Fox Interactive, the parent company of MySpace.

The day saw some lively and sometimes contentious discussions. One safety expert advised parents not to let kids under 17 use services like MySpace except under close parental supervision. Both attorneys general called upon the industry to voluntarily restrict access to only those who are over 16 and to enforce that by using age verification. All this despite the fact that John Cardillo, CEO of Sentry, a leading provider of identity, background and age verification, explained that while verifying the age of adults might be practical, it is impossible to verify the ages of people under 17 because there are no publicly available records that can be used to confirm their identities.

We also heard from John Draper and Christopher Le of the National Suicide Prevention Lifeline who said that referrals from MySpace users have become the largest source of calls to the hotline. Increasingly, kids are using their profiles "to in some ways convey that they had suicidal intent," said Draper in a followup interview. "There is very much the potential for saving lives because the first people to hear about kids at risk are other kids." The federally funded organization is setting up suicide prevention profiles on MySpace, Xanga and Facebook. We don't know how many lives can be saved as a result of referrals through social networks, but it's certainly something that should be thought about by policy makers seeking to restrict teens' access to these sites. This is just one powerful example of how monitoring teen social networking can be much more beneficial to teens than banning it.

The attorneys general who spoke at the Washington meeting are far from the only elected officials calling for government regulation of social networking. As of June 2006, there was already at least one piece of pending federal legislation—the Deleting Online Predators Act of 2006, which would restrict social networking on school and library computers, as if that were actually where the danger lies.

It is easy to understand why politicians would want to regulate MySpace and similar companies. After all the scary news stories, regulation might seem like a way to protect children from "unlawful sexual advances, unlawful requests for sexual favors, or repeated offensive comments of a sexual nature from adults," as the Deleting Online Predators act phrases it. While these elected officials are certainly well-meaning, if we've learned anything from our research for this book, it's that banning social networks not only won't make kids safer, it will actually put them at greater risk.

We understand public officials' concerns and applaud them for thinking about our children's safety, but we also urge them to fund research and carefully study the issues before passing laws or filing lawsuits. To us, it seems too early to pass a law concerning social networking. There's too much we don't know and much research to be done, which makes legislation at this point seem reactive and uninformed.

Susan's Story

Let's end with a story that illustrates the extent to which our teens are continually evolving and why open communication between them and us is a good thing.

"Susan" (not her real name) is an avid MySpace user (her real age is 14). Her parents, who are friends of Larry's, called us because they were concerned Susan was posting too much private information on MySpace, and they didn't understand "this social-networking thing." At the time, she was displaying her full name, lots of pictures of herself, where she went to school, where she hung out after school, and information and pictures from many of her friends. She lied about her age, saying she was over 16 so that she could post a public profile.

Larry had a heart-to-heart chat with Susan, explaining that she really needed to take some steps to protect her privacy. It wasn't a lecture—no scare tactics were used—just an honest discussion of the risks.

We also enlisted Susan's help as we wrote this book and created our Web site, asking her to help us better understand the way teens are using MySpace. Larry and Susan talked for quite a while, with Larry asking most of the questions. It wasn't one of those patronizing conversations where the adult asks questions as a *show* of interest. It was genuine interest because we needed Susan's expertise. She added Larry to her friends list as part of his MySpace training, a very generous act on her part.

During those conversations, something unexpected happened. Susan, who is very reluctant to discuss social networking with her parents or other adults, not only opened up and told us a great deal, but she started to listen as well. The next thing we knew, she had withdrawn some of her personal information, including her last name, posted new photos that were a bit less provocative, and used her real age, which meant that her profile became private.

But then something else happened. The next time we checked in on her profile, she'd changed her display name to include a sexually suggestive four-letter word, and there was more sexually suggestive material on her page. This was a little tough for Larry—while he isn't her parent, he felt he and Susan had made some great progress.

So they had another chat. She told him her profile's new look was all an "inside joke" between her and her friends. He pointed out that, even though her profile was private, her very provocative display name was public and that it might be possible for some of the material on her page to find its way to the wrong people. Susan didn't respond, but she apparently listened *again*, because within a few weeks, she'd changed her disturbing display name and removed some of the age-inappropriate material.

Of course, there's nothing to stop Susan from taking unnecessary risks once again. She, like MySpace and our understanding of social networking, is a work in progress. Fourteen-year-olds, like Web sites, are subject to change without notice. Before we know it, she'll likely be driving a car, going out on real (not just virtual) dates, going to parties where others are perhaps drinking or using drugs, and taking all sorts of other risks. Neither we nor her parents will always be in that car, and we certainly won't be at the parties or along on dates. We can influence her behavior, but we can't control it. And it's important that we not overreact, so that we can continue to have some influence on her decision making.

By far her most effective safeguard, though, is Susan's growing proficiency in fine-tuning a filter that works infinitely better than anything we or her parents could possibly install on her PC. This filter is the software running on the computer between her ears—her own developing critical thinking skills and her ability to make appropriate decisions. Susan doesn't know it, but her experience on MySpace and the adults around her who are listening and gently guiding her are helping her get rid of some of the bugs in that software. Susan's going to be just fine.

You may disagree—and if you do, we hope you'll come talk with us about it. See you online at www.BlogSafety.com!

Index

A

About Me section, 37
account settings, 48–52
    away message, 52
    block user setting, 49
    music settings, 51–52
    profile settings, 49–50
account setup, 28–34
    home page, 32–34
    inviting friends, 31–32
    photo uploads, 30–31
    signup process, 28–29
accounts
    canceling, 61–63, 147–148
    deleting, 148
    setting up, 28–34
Add to Friends link, 68
Add/Edit Photos link, 55
address book, 74–75
adolescents. *See* teenagers
avatars, 6
away message, 52

B

background information, 39–40
bands
    adding profile songs from,
        56–57, 58
    blocking friend requests from, 46
    disabling songs from, 47
Berry, Justin, 116
birthday display option, 46
Blocked Users feature, 49
blocking
    bulletins, 76
    users, 49
Blog Safe mode, 104
blogs, 2, 6, 102–104
    comments on, 104

    privacy options, 46, 103–104
    safety tips for, 133
    setting up, 102–103
BlogSafety.com, 23, 24, 99, 112,
    132, 138
books
    community related to, 89–90
    specifying interests in, 37
bots, 162–163
Boyd, Danah, 16
Boys & Girls Clubs of America, 132
Broughton, Daniel, 113
bulletins, 75–76
    blocking, 76
    posting, 75
    reading, 76, 77
bullying, 114–115, 119–120
Bumiller, Elisabeth, 24

C

calendars, 60–61
canceling accounts, 61–63, 147–148
captions, 55
Cardillo, John, 174
chat rooms, 95–98
    logging on to, 95–96
    parenting points on, 96, 98
child pornography, 128–129
children
    canceling account of, 147
    filtering content for, 146–147
    finding online, 139–142
    monitoring online, 144–146
    parental input for, 132
    safe blogging tips for, 133
classmates, finding, 92–93, 141, 142
college students, 94–95
Comedy community, 90–91